CALLED BY THE GOSPEL

An Introduction to the Christian Faith

MARC KOLDEN

D0898654

AUGSBURG Publishing House • Minneapolis

MANUFACTURED IN THE UNITED STATES OF AMERICA

I have been crucified with Christ; it is no longer I who live but Christ who lives in me; and the life I now live in the flesh I live by faith in the Son of God, who loved me and gave himself for me.

—GALATIANS 2:20

What God does in Christ has a shape; it is an entering into human life, a suffering, a dying, a resurrection from the dead. This lived-out structure of the Christ-deed of grace is identical with the lived-out interior drama of the life of the believer. Faith is participation, and participation is reenactment, and the stages of reenactment are the same as the stages of the Act. . . . Suffering and death are actual reenactments within the life of faith.

—JOSEPH SITTLER

Contents

Preface 7

1. Introduction 9

2. Faith and Understanding 15

3. Humanness and Sinfulness 21

4. Sin and Creation 30

5. Creation and Law 37

6. Law and Gospel 43

7. Our Calling 53

8. Baptism Into Christ 60

9. Baptism Into Christ's Body 68

10. The Church 77

11. The Church's Mission 86

12. The Lord's Supper 95

13. Standing On the Promises 104

Preface

The thinking of many persons has helped to clarify the substance of this book. Those who know his work will see the influence of Gustaf Wingren on many of its pages. Dietrich Bonhoeffer, Reinhold Niebuhr, and Joseph Sittler are the other twentieth century thinkers to whom I am most indebted. And my dependence upon Martin Luther is apparent.

I have written for people in congregations, and much of this material was presented in what was then my own congregation in Helena, Montana, and in other congregations of the American Lutheran Church's Rocky Mountain District. Many of the theological issues were discussed in greater detail with pastors in Idaho, Montana, Washington, and Wyoming.

The initial stimulus to write a basic introduction in the Christian faith came while I was teaching the first time at Luther Theological Seminary in St. Paul, Minnesota. In teaching "core" (required) courses I had to work at the various pieces of the whole, and occasionally I wondered if the individual pieces would fit together.

Upon moving to Montana, I was interested to note that most of the theological issues which concerned pastors were still those of the central Christian doctrines. Here was truly the "core" to which everything else was related. Laypersons too were less interested in fads than in the "solid food" of our theological heritage. Thus most of this was written in response to requests that I speak or teach on a given subject.

I am conscious that my life and work would be much different were it not for many people. Only a few can be mentioned here. Thanks to my parents, Jim and Eunice Grier, who brought me up in the Christian faith. Thanks to the people of Our Redeemer's Lutheran Church in Helena, whom I was privileged to serve as a pastor, and especially to my co-worker there, Pastor Lowell C. Anderson. Thanks also to Bishop Norman G. Wick and to the pastors and congregations of the district whom I also served in the area of continuing education. Finally, to those people with whom I share my life each day, Sally and Michael, many thanks and much love.

MARC KOLDEN

1 · Introduction

What is Christianity? Some say Christianity is a *religion*, or an organized way that a group of people worship and serve God. To this I would say yes, but add that it is not the same as any other religion, for Christians claim that Christianity is true in a way other religions are not. That is not to say that there is no truth in other religions, however.

Some think of Christianity as a *movement*. That certainly seems to be true, but it is much more than a movement, for it deals not only with human activity but has to do with the divine.

Others suggest that Christianity is an *experience* or a set of spiritual experiences. Although experience is part of most people's involvement with Christianity, Christianity is more than individual subjective experiences. Somehow Christianity involves divine reality, and it does so in a way more specifically related to Jesus of Nazareth than "spiritual" might suggest.

Others consider Christianity to be an *organization* of

people who believe or act in certain ways. Organization is involved in being a Christian, and in some ways it might be seen as essential to Christianity, for it expresses the earthly reality of Christianity's claims. But Christianity is much more than only an organization.

Still others describe Christianity as a *way of life*. This is true, but if we speak of Christianity only as a way of life, we may make it into a set of rules for living, and it is not that primarily.

I propose that we should think of Christianity primarily as a *message*. It is a message announcing what God has done, what he is doing, and what he will do. It is a message proclaiming that God has acted decisively in Jesus Christ to redeem the whole world. It is a message with a specific content: the gospel (which means "good news"). Christianity is good news of salvation, embodied in Jesus Christ, whom the Bible calls God's Word.

The Christian Message

If Christianity is a message—a proclamation, an announcement—then several things are implied. The message has a definite *content*. This content is to be found in certain sources: the Bible and great statements of faith, such as the Apostles' Creed.

The message asks for a *response*. It is not neutral information. It claims to have something important for each person to hear. It asks the hearer to believe the content in the sense of trusting in the God who is the subject of the message.

The Christian message starts with Jesus of Nazareth. Jesus was the one promised by the ancient Israelite prophets, descended from the great King David, born of Mary. Nearly two thousand years ago he went about doing good and pro-claiming the reign of God over all of life. He was put to death on a cross because of his actions and teachings, but God raised him from the dead—declaring thereby that Jesus' actions and teachings were true, and that God's love was stronger even than the powers of sin and death.

All people are called to follow this crucified and risen Lord, Jesus Christ. Indeed, as we follow him the form of his life is to take shape in ours, so that we will share with him now in doing good, in suffering, and in death, just as one day we will also share in his resurrection. We live now between his going to be with his Father and his coming again. Now is the time for faith, for being his people in the church, for living as disciples. Now is the time for telling this good news to others and for serving God by serving his creation.

This basic proclamation includes several areas about which we Christians have stated what we think. We believe in the *triune God*, the complex and deep God who is known as Father, Son, and Holy Spirit. We believe that God *creates* and preserves everything that is, and that he guides the affairs of his creation. We believe both in human *goodness*, because we are created and upheld in each moment by God, and in human *sinfulness*, whereby we fail to trust this God and instead act in rebellious and harmful ways. We believe that God reveals his will for his creation in his *law*, which both guides us and accuses us of resisting its demands. We believe in the *gospel* of redemption through Jesus Christ, whereby we are saved from sin, death, and the ultimate power of evil so that we might live as restored creatures. We believe that God calls us through his Spirit to become part of his people, the *church*, where we are nurtured by him through Word and Sacraments and equipped to serve him and bear

witness to his marvelous deeds for us. We believe that we are
called by God also to serve him in all aspects of life in his
world through our *vocations* as family members, as citizens,
workers, church members — wherever we find ourselves.
And we believe in *everlasting life* with God for those who are
united with him through faith in Christ. This hope for the
future is ours solely by God's grace; it is a hope that frees us
to live joyfully and lovingly in the present.

The Point of View

There are several ways that we might organize the teachings
Christians believe. Perhaps the most common way is to include
everything under the three members of the triune God—Father, Son, and Holy Spirit, as the Apostles' Creed might lead
us to do. The advantage of this approach is that it would make
it clear that our faith is in God and that all else we believe
follows from that. I have followed a slightly different path,
however. I have begun thinking from those points in which
our Christian faith comes together with our own lives and
experience—in good times and bad, in work and worship,
in believing and acting. It is my hope that in proceeding this
way the themes of God's creative, redeeming, and sanctifying
work will be held tightly together and the importance for our
daily lives of what we believe about God will be made more
apparent.

I write as one who subscribes to the Lutheran tradition of
understanding the Christian faith. Therefore, I write as one
who seeks to be both *evangelical* and *catholic*. "Evangelical"
comes from the Greek word for gospel, and thus means "good
news"—that we are justified by God's grace through faith in
Jesus Christ and not by what we achieve on our own. Luther-

ans and all other Christians who seek to be evangelical are saying that the center of our life and mission is our belief in this good news.

Yet we also intend to be "catholic." The Latin root of this word refers not to the Roman Catholic Church, but means "universal," applying to all people. Lutherans consider themselves to be a reform movement within the one universal or "catholic" church. Thus, in writing as a Lutheran, I address myself to all Christians and also draw on understandings of faith from the fullness of the Christian heritage. At the same time, I see myself to be continuing the ongoing movement of reform in accordance with the central insights of the Lutheran Reformation.

The title *Called by the Gospel* is taken from a phrase of Martin Luther in his Small Catechism. There he wrote: "I believe that I cannot by my own understanding or effort believe in Jesus Christ or come to him, but the Holy Spirit has *called me by the gospel* . . . ." Called by the message about Christ—this is the central image by which I seek to make sense of the Christian faith. This image gives a particular perspective to each of Christianity's major teachings because the message that calls us is above all a message about death and resurrection. When we are called by this gospel, we are called to die and then to live. This new "itinerary"—death, then life—is just the opposite of our usual way of thinking. It serves notice that understanding the Christian message may lead to conflict with some of our other understandings, which is why our task is so important.

For further reading:

Carlson, Edgar—*The Classic Christian Faith*
Thielicke, Helmut—*I Believe: The Christian's Creed*

QUESTIONS FOR DISCUSSION

1. Do you agree that Christianity is best understood as a message rather than in some other ways? Why or why not?
2. Is the brief description of the Christian message given above adequate as a starting point? How would you change it? Why?
3. If you have some particular questions about Christian faith which you hope to have answered in this book, write them down in the space below so you can return to them later.

2 · Faith and Understanding

Faith seeks understanding. We want to know about the God in whom we believe. Indeed, faith *needs* understanding if it is to direct our lives. The apostle Paul urged Christians to be mature in their thinking. In fact, the whole Bible can be seen as an attempt to express the understanding that under- girds and flows from the faith of God's people.

Faith, that is, trust in God with all one's heart and mind and strength, comes as a gift of God's grace. Understanding, though not coming apart from God's grace (nothing is apart from his grace!), is a human response in which people grasped by God seek to make sense of what faith means and what it leads to in daily life. Understanding our faith is a work, a hu- man activity, a "good work" done for ourselves and for others. We are not saved by our understanding. Rather, understand- ing is one way we communicate and live out the gift of being saved by faith.

Sources for Understanding Faith

In thinking about what Christian faith means we do not start from scratch. Believers have been thinking about their faith and their God for many centuries. The Bible is the primary source for such thinking, and most Christians have said that it is more than just a repository of human thoughts. We say that the books of the Old and New Testaments are understandings which are ultimately true. Indeed, we say that they reveal God to us.

We base our claim that God is revealed to us through the Bible not on any theories about how it was composed or because we can prove the truth of all of its parts (although some try to bolster the Bible's status in these ways). Instead, we say that the Bible reveals God to us because of the witness of countless generations of Christians who have experienced God's revelation of himself through the Bible. The preaching and teaching of the message of the Bible have revealed God to people and brought about faith. The Bible has proved itself to be God's "Word" to us.

Just what the content of that Word of God is will make up the bulk of this book. But for now it should be noted that we also have other sources for helping us understand our faith. These other sources are not as important as the Bible, but they are important. Most are the results of previous centuries of Christian life and thought. We think especially of the great statements of faith (such as the Apostles' and Nicene Creeds) by which Christians have summarized what they believed and what they have rejected from certain other ways of thinking. In addition, there are other writings (sometimes called "confessions" of faith, such as the Augsburg and Westminster Confessions) which have been accepted as explaining accurately the meaning of Christian faith—accepted by the church or simply by gaining a sort of consensus by widespread use. Worship forms and devotional expressions also are ways in which Christian faith has come to understand itself.

All of the ways mentioned above come under the heading of *tradition*. Literally, tradition means "that which has been handed on." In this case, it means the understandings to which faith has given rise in various situations—understandings which people of faith have found to be true and helpful. Some Christians do not value tradition very highly. They think that the Bible is the only valid source for understanding Christian faith. Other Christians consider the Bible itself to be a particularly important part of the tradition; this latter stance usually includes the belief that God is at work among his people since biblical times informing their understandings of faith, which are then expressed in the teachings contained in the tradition.

In this book I will treat the Bible as the primary authority. Yet because I think that our understanding is always conditioned by the context in which we think, and because our context is decisively shaped by our history, I will also pay much attention to the great Christian traditions. They are past ways of making sense of the faith which is evoked by the message of the Bible; it would impoverish our understanding if we were to ignore these traditions.

Approaches to Understanding Faith

Understanding involves more than just learning what has come to be believed in past generations. Faith is not just believing some things about God. Faith is a *relationship* with God; it is a present, living reality. Faith is something that grasps human beings; and we are living, changing, interrelated creatures. Thus, as we construct understandings adequate for today's faith, we will need to take into account the present as well as the past. We need to consider the complexities of human experience as well as the profundity of the God who relates to us.

This includes the fact that no one of us is an isolated individual. Biologically, of course, we are all related to other persons. Simply by observation we can see that most people live and play and work in various groups. But our interrelatedness goes deeper than that. It is inescapable. The fact that we think in words means that our very thoughts are conditioned by the language(s) which we use. The fact that we live in certain societies affects how we understand ourselves in ways over which we have little control. Our race, class, sex, and nationality inevitably affect our understanding—though we are not usually aware of just how much this is so. Finally, even what is held to be "true" is defined by the people who speak of truth. With the rise of modern thought and democratic societies, "truth" also is open to discussion. It can no longer be defined and enforced by authority or superstition. We now need to search for truth and struggle for it.

Thus when faith seeks understanding (and understanding by definition intends to be true), it can no longer simply involve appropriating past understandings. We need to evaluate the adequacy of past as well as of present understandings because we are aware of the extent to which persons "shape" that which they know and hand on. Sometimes our modern understanding has passed over into arrogance, as if only we have the power to decide what is true. And some, in flexing their modern, critical muscles, have rejected all religious claims as mere superstition. But when we realize how quickly the "self-evident truths" of one period end up in the waste-baskets of history, or how quaint the common sense of recent decades seems today, we will be less tempted to claim that present-day canons of truth are automatically better than those of the past.

Yet we Christians today must acknowledge these claims, for we cannot simply deny our own indebtedness to modern thought. But these claims are not all that we acknowledge. We also know that the one who claimed to be the Way, the Truth, and the Life has had a decisive effect on us. Any understanding we formulate now must take Jesus into account also, even and especially if doing so leads us to challenge some of the "truths" of our age.

For further reading:

Gilkey, Langdon—*Message and Existence: An Introduction to Christian Theology*

Jersild, Paul—*Invitation to Faith: Christian Belief Today*

Pannenberg, Wolfhart—*The Apostles' Creed in the Light of Today's Questions*

Tillich, Paul—*Dynamics of Faith*

Truemper, David and Frederick Niedner—*Keeping the Faith: A Guide to the Christian Message*

Wingren, Gustaf—*Credo: The Christian View of Faith and Life*

Note: The books by Gilkey, Jersild, Pannenberg, Truemper and Niedner, and Wingren have sections which correspond to many of the chapters in this book, so they may be valuable helps at several different places. This is true for the books mentioned at the end of Chapter 1 as well.

QUESTIONS FOR DISCUSSION

1. What do you think about using both the Bible and later historical traditions as sources for understanding faith (as described above)?
2. Does it seem correct to think of faith as a *relationship* between the believer and God? How else have you thought of it?
3. What do you think of the idea that faith seeks greater understanding?

3 · Humanness and Sinfulness

*For I do not do the good I want, but the evil I
do not want is what I do. Now if I do what I
do not want, it is no longer I that do it, but sin
which dwells within me.*

—ROMANS 7:19-20

Two Erroneous Views

Sin is a troublesome Christian teaching as well as a troublesome part of our own lives. Ever since I was a small child I
have been taught to say that I am by nature sinful and un-
clean, that I am a poor, miserable sinner, and that there is
no good in me. And I don't like that. Worse yet, it doesn't
seem to me to be true. Yet every Sunday morning we confess
our sins. And I know that the Bible asserts that all people
have sinned and fall short of the glory of God. Indeed, St.
Paul goes to great lengths in the book of Romans to demon-
strate the depth and breadth of human sinfulness.

Yet look at what this has led to: to the belief that people are just no good at all. It has led Christians to widespread pessimism about human abilities and about personal worth. Why? Because in our legitimate concern to say that salvation comes by the grace of God alone, completely apart from any merit on our part, we have overstressed the extent of human sinfulness so that there can be no doubt that salvation is by God's grace—since humans can do nothing good!

But here we are in danger of falling into an ancient heresy —that of equating human nature with sin. It goes back to pre-Christian Greek thinking that downgraded the material world. It was declared to be heretical (that is, a wrong understanding of faith) early in Christian history—as a warning against the Manichaeans, who said that flesh was evil. Yet this heresy has persisted in all sorts of ways so that even in the present we can see evidence of it when we say, "Oh, go ahead and do it; you're only human." Or, "Why not be human?", implying that it is natural to be sinful.

Another example of this cynical and negative view of human nature, which we may think is in agreement with the Christian understanding of sin, is revealed in our almost immediate identification with the "truth" of humorous statements such as "Murphy's Law": "If anything can go wrong, it will!" And the corollaries:

"Nothing is as easy as it looks."

"Everything takes longer than you think."

"Left to themselves, things tend to go from bad to worse."

And the Quantum Revision of Murphy's Law:

"Everything goes wrong all at once."

And O'Toole's Commentary on Murphy's Law:

"Murphy was an optimist!"

My point is that both critics and supporters of the Christian

understanding of sin often have been speaking about a carica-
ture. A doctrine that has real theological significance has led
to psychological and social untruths, so that many Christians
have thought that believing in sin means also to think that
"people are just no good" and that "to err is human." This
has led to the conclusion that therefore we must be pessimistic
about this life, that the only appropriate stance both per-
sonally and socially is a quiet resignation and a profound
discouragement.

Yet such a stance does not ring true with all of our experience, even though it does fit with examples of brokenness
such as death, divorce, racism, sexism, poverty, and political
oppression as well as the many minor absurdities of daily life.
Some of our experiences are positive and reveal real promise
on the part of people and society. These days there is much
talk among Christians about the human potential movement
and possibility thinking. This leads some to reject the view
of sin described earlier as having been overdone, demoraliz-
ing, and self-defeating. The idea arises instead that "if you
think you can do something, you can."

As an example of this erroneous view, I will never forget
"possibility thinker" Robert Schuller's remarks at former
Vice-President Hubert Humphrey's funeral service. Schuller
pointed down from the pulpit at the casket containing Humphrey's body and he began to commend to all of us the "big
C" that had been so helpful to Humphrey throughout his life
and especially in his dying days. I was cautiously hopeful that
at least in the face of death Schuller would point us to Christ,
the "big C." But no. The "big C" that supposedly was so
much help to Humphrey even in death was "Courage." Yes,
Hubert, I thought, you just be brave in that casket; that will
help a lot!

If I had to pick one of these false alternatives, I would rather take Murphy than Schuller, but my point is that we do not have to choose between these two. What they are illustrating or rejecting is a one-sided view of sin, not the classical Christian understanding. Yet many of us think that we are stuck with either the supposed negative thinking of the tradition or the naive optimism being propounded today.

A Better Way

There is help both from the Bible and from the great thinkers and statements of the tradition. When they speak of sin they do so *paradoxically*. A paradox is a category for describing the fact that sometimes we must say two things which are contradictory in order to say the whole thing, in order to account for all the data.

The way in which the Bible speaks of humans and sin (especially in Gen. 1-3 and Rom. 7—and I am summarizing drastically) is to say that God is good and creates us good, and therefore we are not *necessarily* sinful. Yet it also says that all people are *in fact* sinful, inevitably and universally. And at this point we have only begun to see the paradox! Human beings are shown as being tempted to sin by a power far greater than we are, and are even said to be under the rule of sin, death, and the devil—and yet *we* are said to be responsible for sinning! Along with this, the Bible constantly urges us to love one another and to act justly and creatively (as if we could) while at the same time telling us that all people are sinful and cannot do these things. Finally, to make it even more monstrous, it is said that all this came about outside of our own individual lives ("in Adam") and yet we are judged guilty for it.

About this radical and paradoxical description of humans and sin in the Bible (it is usually called the doctrine of "Original Sin"), the philosopher Pascal wrote: "Certainly nothing offends us more rudely than this doctrine, and yet without this mystery, the most incomprehensible of all, we are incomprehensible to ourselves" (*Pensees*, 434). In other words, in order to understand what faith knows about humans and sin, we must say something more complex than simply either "We are no good" or "We are only good."

In much of the history of the Christian church this paradoxical teaching has not been fully held. Often what was said was that, in effect, humans are partly good and partly sinful. This led to the conclusion that salvation is partly by grace (since we are partly sinful) and partly by our doing good works (which we can do, at least to a point, since we are partly good). The problem with this is that it would mean that salvation is not by grace alone, apart from works of law —and this clearly contradicts the Bible (see, for example, Romans 3 and Ephesians 2:8-9).

Essentially Good and Totally Depraved

The Reformers of the sixteenth century, especially Martin Luther and John Calvin, emphasized the paradox of the Christian understanding of sin in a way that few others have. The Lutheran Confessions state that human nature is in every moment created good; that is, we are *essentially* good ("essentially" here means that which is at the heart of what it means to be human). If that were not true, it was argued, why would Christ have taken on himself our human nature or why would God have wanted to save it? Or, it was asked, if the human body were merely sinful, why would the creeds insist on the resurrection of the *body* after death? Human nature, therefore, is essentially good. Though present in humanity, evil is not a part of what it means to be human; evil is something that adheres to the human, but it is not at the heart of what it means to be human. This is similar to the Nicene Creed's assertion that Jesus was truly human, even though he was without sin.

It is clear that the tradition makes a distinction between humanness and sinfulness. But are we then simply to downplay sin as incidental and only stress human goodness? By no means!

Faithful to the Bible, the Reformers went on to speak of the "total depravity" of human beings. Now at first glance that phrase seems as one-sidedly negative as the first erroneous view of sin that was criticized earlier. What could be more depraved than being *totally* depraved? But this is another example of a theological distinction being taken as a psychological or personal description. The concept of total depravity was intended to be used against those who argued that there was some "spark" of divinity or goodness or reasoning power remaining in us unaffected by sin. No, said the Reformers, there is no part of us unaffected by sin by which we can do something to help in our salvation or can cooperate with God. Every part of us is affected; we are *totally* depraved.

However, to say that no part of us escapes sin is not to say that we human beings have no good in us. Rather, it is to say that in every way, in every aspect of our being, and in every act, while all things come to us as God's good gifts, there is always *also* in us and in everything we do an aspect of rebellion against God. Even in our highest acts, such as loving someone else, there will always be an aspect of serving ourselves. "Depraved" means "perverted", after all; literally, it means turning something good to an evil purpose, so that something intended to be *used* is *ab-used*. This view of sin says that our use of good means toward ends that are permeated by mixed motives and purposes is total.

A Realistic Approach

Note that in speaking this way the good in us (and in all people, including nonbelievers) is not denied, despite our constant defecting. Rather, human goodness is always *qualified* in a highly realistic way. This understanding of human goodness and sinfulness is realistic (that is, true to experience, if we give it some thought) because if we do not take sin with utter seriousness, we will surely misunderstand ourselves and events in our world, and then we will be ill-equipped to enter into the challenges set before us in life. If we do not take sin seriously we may be hampered by holding naive, overly-optimistic expectations of people and organizations. This will at best lead to constant disappointment and at worst it will leave us unable to address effectively the deep-seated personal and social problems that confront us. In parallel fashion, if we do not take human goodness with full seriousness, we may simply resign ourselves to failure—letting the world "go to the devil", relinquishing our own responsibility, and ending in cynicism.

For example, this understanding of sin would lead us to see as *one aspect* of the energy crisis and food shortage in the world that God's judgment is being exercised on those of us in the industrial nations for our wanton misuse of resources. "Judgment" and "crisis" are the same word in the Greek New Testament, meaning a time of reckoning, a time when we are confronted with the results of sin. We know further that in the Bible judgment is not considered to be an end in itself, but is a working out of God's wrath for the sake of his mercy. Therefore, if we do not take sin seriously at this point we will miss many of the more profound implications of human perversity revealed by these shortages, which simply cry out to be dealt with—by judgment and mercy.

Or, again, in the face of any incident or situation, if we remember that all people are always *also* sinful (created good in every moment and yet always *also* in every act rebelling against God), we will know that no person or cause is pure, not even our own. Nothing on earth can be identified through and through with the work of God.

Among other things, taking sin with such seriousness will help us understand the guilt of "good" people and of those who are "intelligent" and "powerful." Reinhold Niebuhr speaks of the "equality of sin and inequality of guilt." He is referring to the fact that although all people are always also sinful, some have more actual guilt because they have more power or money or education with which to exercise their freedom both in doing good and in doing evil. The Christian understanding of sin is a realistic view which helps us to make sense of daily life as we experience it.

For further reading:

    Gilkey, Langdon—*Shantung Compound*
    Niebuhr, Reinhold—*The Nature and Destiny of Man*, Vol.
      I, Chapters 5-10.

QUESTIONS FOR DISCUSSION

1. If human sinfulness is overemphasized, what are the dangers?
2. If human goodness is overemphasized, what are the dangers?
3. Is the way of understanding goodness and sinfulness outlined above satisfactory to you? Why or why not?
4. Do you think the "realistic" approach might be helpful in particular situations in your life or the life of our nation? In what ways?

4 · Sin and Creation

Creation is repeated in every birth; the Fall is the egocentric attempt by every man to guarantee his own safety.

—GUSTAF WINGREN

It became clear in the previous chapter that we cannot talk about sin correctly without also speaking of the creation of everything by God. That the world is God's creation is part of what Christians believe, but it is a part often ignored or misunderstood.

God's creative work is *ignored* when we treat people and the material world as if they had no referent beyond themselves—as if parents themselves create human life, which then exists for seventy years or so and perishes, or as if the material world has no value except as it serves human beings. Clearly, this utilitarian or secular approach is widespread in our day, so that an understanding of the meaning of creation will be opposed to what is perhaps the majority viewpoint in our society.

30

God's creative work is *misunderstood* if it is thought that once upon a time God made everything and now it simply goes along on its own. Many sincere Christians seem to have thought that the opening chapters of the Bible are a description only of how the world *began*. Yet this portion of the Bible (Gen. 1-2) as well as other portions concerned with creation (for example, Job, Isa. 40-66, many of the Psalms) are primarily interested not in how the world began in the past but in confessing that the *present* world can be rightly understood only by seeing that it is always dependent on the creativity of God.

The Bible's Treatment of Sin and Creation

The importance of the biblical notion that God's creative work is not only at the beginning but also is ongoing and important for every moment leads us to reexamine as well a certain misunderstanding of sin. Those who have thought of Genesis 1-2 as a literal report of the beginning of time and of the forming of human beings have tended to see Genesis 3 as a literal description of the beginning of sin. I call this the "chronological fallacy" in Christian thinking: it says, *first* there was creation, *then* there was sin. If we think in this wooden way, the creation fades into the remote past and sin seems to be the major reality for us and our world, since it came after creation. This thinking tends to make us value redemption as the cure for sin more highly than creation. Such a view has dangerous consequences, for it encourages us to think of redemption and living the Christian life as a flight away from the created world, not recognizing the good that is in the world even in the midst of sin because of God's ongoing creative work.

Genesis 1-3 are part of a larger body of writings. Scholars think that we must hold together all of Genesis 1-11 —the "prehistory" of the Bible. In reading all eleven chapters we see the rhythm of God's ongoing creative work and people's ongoing defecting in the midst of living out the created goodness and freedom God gives them. If "Adam" does in fact mean "humankind", then the story of Adam and Eve and God and Satan in the garden is a profound story telling us not only something about the past but about us in the present as well. It tells us (1) that we belong to God, (2) that it is good to be a creature, (3) that we are both one with the created order and yet set over it as stewards, (4) that we are limited in our understanding of and our trust in God and thus are liable to temptation and rebellion, and (5) that in fact we do, over and over again, reject God's word and seek to be our own little gods.

What is needed is to take these stories "seriously but not literally," as Reinhold Niebuhr said. If we see clearly that the story of Adam is also our story, we will be less inclined to ignore the notions of God's creative work and of our sinfulness. In Adam, Paul wrote, we *all* sin (Rom. 5:12). It is not simply that each of us sins like Adam did (that view treats Adam only as an individual and not as symbolic of humankind). If that were the case, someone might think that he or she did not *have* to sin. Yet both the Old and New Testaments clearly portray sin as both inevitable and universal ("All have sinned." Rom. 3:23).

Further, just as Adam's sin was not portrayed as only his own free act, but as a complicated situation involving Eve and the tempter, the creation and God's prohibition, so also the Christian tradition has spoken of sin not only as individual actions but also as a complex corporate condition. "We are in bondage to sin," and "We have sinned against God by thought, word and deed." The individual sins flow from the situation or condition. And yet, if we say only that, it sounds as if sin is not our responsibility but is simply passed on to us (genetically or by our environment). With the Psalmist, we must also say, "*I* have sinned and done what is evil in thy sight" (Ps. 51:4).

This discussion of sin is an attempt both to make sense of the Bible's unsystematic treatment of sin and to do justice to our own experience. If we demand complete clarity, if we seek to dissolve the paradox, we risk losing part of the Christian teaching.

Interpreting Sin and Creation Today

Sin is a *relational* term. It speaks of the relationship between God and people. Several words have been used to describe sin: rebellion, estrangement, wrongdoing, despair, pride, brokenness, and falling short. Each of these words portrays both a failure of the person(s) involved and a sense of powerlessness or of being caught by something beyond oneself that one does not seem to be able to resist.

Thus we can say that we know about sin to some degree from our own experience. To get at is full radicality, however, we must go beyond our own experience, for our experience is always ambiguous. This is why, finally, sin is something in which Christians *believe*. We "confess" our sin, just as we confess our faith. That is, we agree with God's word. In this case, we agree with his judgment on us—that we are sinful (see Ps. 51:4). On the basis of the evidence alone we would not be sure of our sinfulness; we would always be justifying our actions in some way so as to avoid seeing our sinfulness.

When we agree with God's judgment we begin to see that the root of all sin is *unbelief*. Unbelief means not trusting God with all our heart and mind and strength. The other side of this coin is that we trust instead in something or someone else (someone has called this a "godlet"). Adam did not believe God's judgment that it was good to be a creature; he wanted to be like God and decide for himself about good and evil. Or as Paul puts it in Romans 1:25, we have worshiped the creature rather than the Creator. Confessing our sin and believing (God's word) that we are sinful is already a move from sin, away from unbelief, because it is taking God at his word.

It is important to relate this understanding of sin back again to God's creative work, for if we fail to do this some of the old misunderstandings of sin may allow us to continue in some of the old misunderstandings of creation. Thinking of both sin and creation as ongoing aspects of the relationship between God and people is vitally important for the ways in which Christians make sense of life in the present and in the immediate future. One wrong way is to think of God's creative work as *progress*. Some have thought that somehow things are getting better and better. This illusion of inevitable progress, fortified by religious underpinnings, may lead to a failure on the part of Christians to take responsibility for actions because of the assumption that everything will turn out all right anyway. Or it may lead to a fatalism which can be wrong and even dangerous (for example, driving recklessly in the belief that nothing can happen to you until your "number is up"). Or it may lead us to see failure or weakness as sin.

It is more accurate to say that the Bible understands history to be characterized by *change* rather than by progress. There are certainly changes throughout history, but there is no clear progress toward any goal going on in history itself. Similarly, there is not clear regress either; things are not inevitably getting worse. When Jesus said that his kingdom was not of this world, and when he warned of judgment and declared the need for divine salvation, he was pointing out that our hope does not lie with progress in history itself.

A second way Christians have often misapplied the teaching about God's creation of the world is to say that the forms, institutions, and laws present in the created world are given once and for all and are therefore *unchangeable*. Lutheran Christians have been especially prone to argue in this way, going back to the Reformers' arguments for the validity of the "order of creation" as these were interpreted in Lutheran state churches. Here we need to remember that the Reformers were arguing against the Medieval Roman Catholic notions that it is more righteous to live a religious life apart from the world and also that the church is to rule the other areas of society. Against this, the Reformers said that each order of creation, for example, family, business, government, has its own validity by virtue of its creation by God. Therefore, the church ought not to rule the other areas of society, and therefore the call to the religious life of the monasteries and cloisters is not better than other callings.

The *value* of the Reformers' emphasis is in their affirmation of all of life on the basis of God's ongoing creative work. The problem is that the orders of creation in effect when and where the claims were made tended to become definitive. Thus this view, intended to honor God's ongoing creative work, often ended up by conserving the forms of a past era and justifying the status quo——usually in self-serving and oppressive ways (condoning slavery, obedience to tyrants, male domination, and other forms of violence). Such thinking is actually based on a static view of creation, more akin to deism's idea of God as the one who started the world as a watchmaker winds up a clock than to the lively notion of God in the Bible.

Martin Luther sums up the biblical view accurately, I think, when he says about God being the Creator that "to create is perpetually to make anew." If that is the case, Christians who serve God in his world are liberated for radically new actions as well as for conserving actions. Making changes in forms and institutions may then be seen to be precisely what is desirable and in accordance with God's will. In any case, the emphasis is on our own freedom, responsibility, and creativity—and not simply on obedience to authority or to the status quo. To quote Luther further, "A good act is one that is good for our neighbor." Thus doing a good act demands both selflessness and intelligence about what my neighbor might need in each situation. Neither the Creator nor the creature can settle for a static notion of reality and action. How this can be understood will concern us in the next chapter.

For further reading:

    Bonhoeffer, Dietrich—*Creation and Fall*
    Westermann, Claus—*Creation*

QUESTIONS FOR DISCUSSION

1. Does the suggestion to take the biblical stories of creation and fall "seriously but not literally" offer a good way of understanding them? Why or why not?
2. What do you think of the idea that sin is something a Christian *believes* in?

5 · Creation and Law

"The Law is the most excellent of all things in the world."

—MARTIN LUTHER

The Law for All People

"To create is perpetually to make anew," said Luther, in explaining the biblical understanding of God's creative work. In each moment, God is involved in upholding what exists or it would cease to be. And in each moment God is involved in the new things that come to be.

The Bible does not portray God's creative work as erratic or chaotic in its novelty, however. God's creative work expresses his own will and purposes. Since he is a God of love, he creates out of love and in the hope of increasing love. Since he is a God of peace and justice, he intends for that which he creates to exist in peace and harmony.

The biblical word that expresses God's creative will for

37

his creation is *law*. We could say that law is the creative will of God, and the purpose of the law is to preserve, direct, and enhance creation. Law in this sense deals with the natural or social or political expression of God's will for the world and its people.

Theologians have spoken of this as the "first use" of the law. It is the way in which God guides or compels us to be part of his ongoing creative work. Since it follows from God's ongoing work, law in this sense should not be seen as static or unchanging or necessarily as negative or harsh. Nor should law in its common-sense or first use be thought of as something that only religious people know. If the law is God's creative will, expressed in his work of creation, then all people potentially can be aware of the law. As St. Paul said, it is written on the hearts of all people (Rom. 2:15). Thus we are not only talking about laws which are written out, but also about those which are "built in" to the world itself. Reactions of guilt or of sympathy in certain situations, for example, might be understood as ways in which God's will influences us.

In terms of faith, the most important thing to remember about the law in its first use is that it applies to the created world and to all its creatures. It keeps the creation functioning lovingly and justly. The law is something God gives out of love. His love comes prior to the law. Our keeping the law, therefore, is not intended to be a means by which we are to gain God's approval or favor. Thinking that way is "legalism," that is, thinking that God's love for us depends on our doing certain things the law requires. The reason God gives us the law is to lead us to treat other people and our world properly—for our own good and for theirs. We need to keep that straight.

The Law and the Christian Life

Christians have not always kept that straight. Some have thought that keeping some sort of law made them better or more acceptable to God (whether the Ten Commandments or "Thou shalt not smoke, thou shalt not chew; thou shalt not be with folks who do.") This is nonsense, according to the Bible. Worse than that, it is heresy, for it makes our relationship with God dependent on what *we* do instead of on what God does.

Because of this heresy, other Christians have tried to get rid of the law altogether. The Bible says that Christ is the end of the law (Rom. 10:4), and some Christians have decided that they don't need any law after they become Christians. However, the statement that Christ is the end of the law needs to be interpreted carefully. St. Paul, who wrote that sentence, has other things to say as well, and these would lead us to believe that Christ ends the law in terms of anyone thinking that he or she can gain acceptance in God's eyes by living according to the law. But when Paul gives illustrations of the sorts of things faithful Christians will do in living according to faith, these look very much like the summary of the law Jesus endorses: that is, loving God above all things and our neighbors as much as ourselves.

Since Martin Luther was one who had harsh criticisms of the law, and since he often said things such as "the Christian is the perfectly free lord of all, subject to none"—in this way illustrating the complete freedom from doing good works to please God which the forgiveness of sins grants us—we need to consider his statements in relation to any positive emphases about the law. Luther makes a sharp distinction between speaking of our life in relationship to God and in relationship to the world and other people. He insists that in relationship to God, our keeping the law is useless and dangerous, for here everything depends on God's gracious love toward us. As long as we make our doing something a condition for God's loving us, we are sinning—we are not taking God at his word that he loves us and forgives us freely for Christ's sake. In this context the law is a terrible thing and we should have nothing to do with it.

In this world and with other people, however, Luther says that the law is a marvelous thing, the best part of creation. Indeed, by keeping the law a person can become righteous in the ordinary sense of being a good person in the eyes of other people. Even those who do not willingly keep the law, but do so out of fear of punishment or because of threats or force, keep the law in an earthly sense and do good things. The point here is not about their motivation but about results; for example, taxes are paid, people do not steal, murder, and cheat, drivers do not speed.

Seeing the importance of making the law separate from God's approval of us and keeping it central in our living in the world will help us value properly both God's free grace and the world we live in. Understanding this life and everything we do as part of God's ongoing creative work, guided by his law, will affect the way we face each day and each situation. It will give importance even to things that seem trivial, such as casual acts of kindness. It may make us see that acting justly or honestly or compassionately is important, instead of just living each day for ourselves. For since everything depends on God and nothing happens apart from his ongoing creativity, in each moment we will be dealing with him also. Thus we will seek to relate to everyone and to everything in ways appropriate to their relationship to God. Thinking in this way is humbling, to be sure, but also exciting.

Seeing how important the doctrine of creation is for Christian faith helps us to understand the truth of Anglican Archbishop Temple's statement that "Christianity is the most *materialistic* of all religions." Its chief concern is the preservation and salvation of the created world.

From this it follows that if sin is a perversion of creation, then salvation will be the healing or restoration of creation. If in sinning the creature rebels against the status of being a creature (Adam and Eve did not accept God's judgment on creation that "it is good" but sought instead "to be like God"), then in salvation we are made new *creatures*. We are completed and fulfilled, but as creatures. The work of Christ fulfills God's word in creation: "Let us make man in our image."

In other words, the Bible's view that God's creating is the basis for everything else will help us to understand the claims made about Jesus: that he was truly *human;* that he came because God so loved the *world;* that he came that we might have abundant *life*; and that we hope in Christ for the resurrection of our *bodies*. Jesus dramatically enacted what was always true of God: that he is a "down-to-earth" God. This helps us to see that our sin is in seeking to flee from the earth, which is God's and which is where God intends us to be. Therefore, Christian faithfulness will anchor us in creation, as creatures, living in accordance with God's law. But this is to get ahead of ourselves, because the law has another use, a use we know all too well.

For further reading:
    Wingren, Gustaf—*Creation and Law*

QUESTIONS FOR DISCUSSION

1. Do you agree that people know something of God's law even apart from faith and that it is "built in" to creation?
2. Do you think it is helpful to use God's law in giving direction to our Christian life? Do you see any risks in doing this?
3. What do you think of the idea that salvation is the restoration and fulfillment of creation?

6 · Law and Gospel

The Lord kills and brings to life; he brings down to Sheol and raises up.

—1 SAMUEL 2:6

The Second Use of the Law

If the world were perfect and if we were without sin, we would all live in harmony according to God's law. In fact, we would not even need God's law for we would naturally do what is right and faithful. Because of sin, the law was made explicit—to guide and compel us to do what is right.

If it were only that simple! Because of sin, even when we know the law, we do not always keep it. In fact, if the truth were known, we never keep it fully. As we realize this, we may also realize a "second use" of God's law: it reveals our sin to us. It shows us what we have not done and it reveals our resistance to keeping the law even in those instances when we "keep it" on an outward level.

43

The Protestant Reformers said that "the law always accuses." They were arguing against the decadent religion of their time which suggested that one could gain God's favor by keeping certain laws. Most of the laws in question were not even the great commandments which deal with our lives in the world. Instead, most of them were religious requirements about church attendance, fasting, and giving money which did no good at all for one's neighbor but which supposedly did something for a person's relationship to God (that is, for one's salvation).

Martin Luther, who grew up and entered the priesthood under this teaching, discovered that even when he kept all of these "laws" he never felt as if God accepted him. The various laws only revealed to him his inadequacies when applied to his conscience and to the question of his worthiness in the eyes of God. Thus he concluded that in relationship to God, "the law always accuses."

This experience helped Luther to see the biblical evidence that the law was never intended to be a means of securing God's favor. When the Ten Commandments were given, they were given *after* God had rescued the Israelites from bondage in Egypt to give his people, whom he already loved, some means of preserving their nation and living in such a way as to honor their God. While sometimes God's people got this mixed up, both before the time of Christ and after, it is quite clear that St. Paul's summary statements that salvation is by God's grace and not by our keeping the law express the overwhelming consensus of the Bible.

When Christians speak about law and gospel together they refer to this second use of the law—its accusing use. Here the law is perceived as being against us: it reveals our sin, convicts us, drives us to despair, crushes us, and finally kills us. The law which guides us (first use) at the same time accuses us and reveals the depth of our sinfulness (second use). The amazing thing is that the law is not God's last word. There is another word which reveals that God himself was at work in the law—working to put to death the defiant sinner so that he could raise us to life again as his own creature. This new word from God is gospel—the good news about Jesus Christ who came to forgive our sin, liberate us from bondage, restore our hope, end our warfare with God, and give us new life.

The Central Paradox

As with sin, we must also speak of salvation paradoxically. We must say two things that seem to be contradictory to get at the reality.

The Bible usually speaks of salvation by contrasting things in terms of old and new: the old age of sin and the new age of Christ; the old creation and the new creation; and the old Adam and the new Adam (Christ). And somehow it is not as if the old had completely passed away and the new has come, nor as if the old age is still with us and we await the new age to come. Rather, the old and the new are said to exist simultaneously. The new age has begun but the old age lives on.

Sometimes this is pictured as a battle—with Jesus Christ, the bringer of the new age, fighting with Satan, the ruler of the old age. Sometimes it is pictured as a conflict within a person—in which my old, sinful self, loyal to Adam and to the devil, is at war with my new, forgiven self, loyal to Christ. Whatever the picture, the danger is that we will let go of the tension involved in the paradox and settle for a little bit of old and a little bit of new. To combat this, St. Augustine, about four hundred years after Christ, used a helpful phrase to describe the Christian person—*simul iustus et peccator* (at the same time righteous and sinful). The Reformers took over this phrase and we too may find it helpful even though paradoxical.

In terms of our relationship to God, it is not the case that each of us is at the same time partially sinful and partially righteous, even though on a common sense level this seems to be the way it is. Instead, we might look at it this way: being righteous is like being pregnant—you either are or you aren't. You cannot be a little bit pregnant, even though we sometimes talk that way about a woman in the early stages of pregnancy. So, too, if our righteousness depends on God's favor toward us, and if his favor is certain because of his saving work in Christ, then we are 100% righteous. Or consider another analogy. In the days of kings it used to be said that one could not go part way in opposing a king. If you started a movement to get rid of the king (in a system which did not allow for that), then you had to kill the king or he would kill you. By analogy, if God is God and if we oppose that (if we want to be God), this resistance is 100% since there cannot be two Gods.

Thus this is truly a paradox and cannot be resolved in mathematical terms. A Christian is totally righteous and totally sinful at the same time. Because we will remain totally sinful until the day we die, we always need the law to reveal our sin, accuse us, and put us to death. And for the same reason we continually need the gospel to forgive our sin, deliver us from evil, and raise us to new life. The paradox will only be resolved after our physical death and final resurrection when Christ will be all in all.

The Central Teaching of the Christian Faith

This paradox leads us to the central point of the Christian message, the article of faith "by which the church stands or falls", namely, *justification by faith*. To be justified means to be counted as being righteous. St. Paul quotes Genesis 15:6 to make this point: "Abraham believed God and it was reckoned to him as righteousness" (Rom. 4:3). This does not mean that we are counted righteous *because* of our believing; that would make our act of believing into another good work for which we might take credit. The Bible is clear that we are "justified by faith in Christ and not by works of law" (see Gal. 2:16 and Eph. 2:8-9).

The point is that our being counted righteous is God's *unconditional* declaration of his love for us, his acceptance of us "while we were yet sinners" (Rom. 5:8), and his forgiveness for our sins. This declaration he made when he took our flesh on himself in the man Jesus Christ and died on the cross for our sake. And when in Christ God overcame the powers of sin, death, and the devil, he promised us that Jesus' victory is for us as well. This promise has no conditions; it is the last judgment ahead of time. It simply says that "the crucified one lives for you." When we hear this, we say with Paul, "I have been crucified with Christ! It is no longer I who live but Christ who lives in me; and the life I now live in the flesh I live by faith in the Son of God, who loved me and gave himself for me" (Gal. 2:20).

Our faith in this promise is not something *we do*; it is not having the proper attitude or opinion about this promise or about Jesus Christ. Faith follows from hearing the promise. It is our whole life lived as persons judged irrevocably worthy by God himself, whose judgments are sure. Faith comes simply by our hearing this wholly unconditional promise. This is not surprising if we remember that the whole purpose of Christ's coming was to create faith because it is unbelief which is our sin and which leads us to oppose God. To overcome our unbelief God's Spirit creates faith through the word about Christ. As long as we want to "do our part" it is the "old Adam" in us continuing to oppose God's word. As Gerhard Forde has said, the point of our being justified by faith alone apart from works of law is that when we do nothing God gets *everything*, all of us, and we are saved.

The Lust For More Than Grace Alone

This way of thinking runs counter to certain Christian traditions, which hold that one can become more holy (or "sanctified") by working at it throughout one's life. Indeed, a few Christian groups have taught that a person can reach perfection in this life. A popularization of this position has it that "every day in every way we are getting better and better."

While there is clearly something appealing and even biblical-sounding in thinking that believing in Christ should make us better persons, there are dangers which seem to keep arising with this way of thinking. The first danger is that this approach easily degenerates into legalism—that is, making our relationship with God depend on our keeping certain laws— and then we may even begin to take pride in how good we are becoming. In contrast, the Bible seems to indicate that the Christian, like Paul himself, will be surprised by any goodness which he or she finds and quickly give credit for it to God's grace. To put it another way, perfect or true humanity belongs to Christ and to the age to come. Nothing that promises it now is Christian.

A second danger in concentrating on becoming better and better is less a doctrinal one than an experiential one. If progress on a historical level is not apparent, neither is it so on a personal level. The reality here also is change, not progress. And if we think that progress is demanded and yet we do not find it (even the most "holy" among us may be racists, alcoholics, or spouse-beaters), then we are liable to be unhappy and disillusioned persons, to say the least, and we may end up with severe emotional disturbances in some cases. For the law always accuses, finally. If we include in our practice of Christian faith some laws about getting better and better, they will "get" us—later, if not sooner.

To be sure we remember this point, it might be more help-ful to say that a Christian gets worse and worse every day! "Growing in grace" means realizing each day more fully that we are totally dependent on God's grace.

This tendency in all of us to want to do our part and to resist the promise that we are justified by faith in Christ is what I call "the lust for more than grace alone." The main characteristic of this tendency is that *we* want to do something or *we* want to have a more real and vibrant religious life or *we* want to have some tangible assurance that God is working in our lives. In other words, we are lusting for *more than the promise* that God loves us unconditionally and will continue to do so forever.

I use the word "lust" because lust is an inappropriate desire or passion for something, such as sex, money, or power. Such things are not bad in themselves, just as religious assurance and a real sense of God's presence are not bad in themselves. What is wrong is our lust for them—our wanting to have them for ourselves *at all costs*. Our lust for more than grace alone is the height of sin right in the middle of our religious life.

The tragedy is that if we insist on more we will get less, for we will be left to our own devices. And when it comes to the ultimate things of life—such as salvation, death, tragedy, joy, meaning—we will be helpless if we are left on our own. The problem of sin is our ego—that is, our too-great concern for ourselves. "Grace alone" says that the way out of this dilemma is not the "I", not the self, but God's forgiveness of our self-centeredness. When we want more than that, it is our ego reasserting itself. It is sin, not faith. The Christian says, "Not I, but Christ who lives in me" (Gal. 2:20). *I* am the problem. It is I who need to die with Christ so that I may also be raised with him.

When we say the central point of the Christian message is "justification by faith" (or "grace alone") we are not only saying that this doctrine is more important than other teachings to be believed, or that it is first among equals. What is at stake is the very essence of what we understand Christianity to be. It is not that God arbitrarily decided to save us by grace alone, or that the Bible tells us to believe this, as if there were no substantive reason for it. There is a reason, and the reason is this: God's free grace for us is intended to free us *from* concern about ourselves and to free us *for* being concerned about this world and other people. We are set free by grace to live as faithful creatures. We *are not* to spend our time seeking our own pleasure or our own spiritual fulfillment; we *are* to spend our time getting on with the business of living—freed by grace and seeking nothing more.

This is what is meant when it is said that the gospel comes to free us from the law or that Christ ends the reign of law in our relationship with God. As it frees us from the accusation and condemnation of the law and from our frantic attempts to make something of ourselves, it also frees us *for* the law in its first use—for our neighbor. This may not give us any edge on goodness over our nonbelieving friends, since we are still forgiven sinners, but we will at least be aware that the demands and compulsions on us to serve other people are the demands and compulsions of God on us.

This brings us to the strange notion of Christian freedom: that freedom for the Christian is resuming our obedience under the law in the world. But it is a strange notion only for those whose understanding of Christian faith ignores creation as a basic category. If faith is thought to be an escape from the world or from the body, then to hear that the gospel returns us to the world and to the body will sound strange and perverse. But if God's creative work is most basic of all and if his saving work is in continuity with his creative work, then *Christian* freedom will be related to creation and therefore to law. Doing anything one wants is "license." Perfect freedom is found in service to the God of love. The law binds us. The gospel sets us free from the law's bondage into the service of the one in whose image we are being made. *How* this happens is our next topic.

For further reading:

Forde, Gerhard—*Where God Meets Man*, esp. Chapter 4
Forde, Gerhard—*Justification By Faith—A Matter of Death and Life*
Gritsch, Eric and Jenson, Robert—*Lutheranism,* esp. Chapters 3-5
Knutson, Kent S.—*His Only Son Our Lord*, esp. Chapter 4

QUESTIONS FOR DISCUSSION

1. Martin Luther thought that the ability to distinguish between law and gospel was the most important task of the
   Christian thinker. Why do you think Luther said that?
2. Do you see any problems with thinking that God accepts
   and forgives people without conditions? What is good
   about such a teaching?
3. Can you think of examples of people or groups who are
   not satisfied with grace alone and who wish to add something else to the Christian gospel?

7 · Our Calling

When God calls a man, he bids him come and die.
— DIETRICH BONHOEFFER

The Idea of Vocation

The Bible speaks of God "calling" us to be his people, to believe in him and to serve him. The particular ways in which we respond to his call often have been designated as our "callings." Since this is an ancient idea, and since the language of western Christianity during most of its first fifteen hundred years was Latin, the Latin word for calling, *vocatio,* came to be the usual way of speaking of this notion. From this we get our word "vocation."

Sometimes vocation can refer primarily to specific service to the church, as in the Roman Catholic tradition, in which vocation usually refers to the clergy or to those in religious orders. Or, in a secular sense, we often use the word vocation about *any* occupation—as in Vocational-Technical Schools.

53

Instead of either of these usages, I will follow the Protestant tradition of using vocation to refer specifically to our being called by God to serve him in whatever occupation or circumstance we choose or happen to be in. Any task or situation can be a vocation if the person understands that he or she is serving God thereby. Thus to have a Christian vocation does not mean that one has to serve the institutional church or be doing something religious.

Our calling to be Christians restores and transforms our callings to be creatures, and to be workers, students, family members, citizens, and the like. This follows our previous line of thought whereby the gospel frees us from the law's condemnation for living in accord with the law. The notion of vocation gives specificity to how Christian faith will be lived out in daily situations.

An almost immediate result of the rise of this view of vocation in the sixteenth century Reformation was the new validity given to "secular" work. Some historians have traced the rise of capitalism and the modern industrial state to this so-called "Protestant ethic." While many other factors clearly were involved in these developments, and while Christian underpinnings of various enterprises were often questionable, it is apparent that the idea of vocation allowed people to speak positively about their participation in a wide range of activities that previously had not seemed important for living the Christian life.

Monastic vows of poverty, celibacy, and obedience were repudiated by the Protestant Reformers and the ideals they represented ("the counsels of perfection" directed at only a select group of Christians) were replaced by more worldly pursuits—but still to the glory of God! The possibilities of corruption present in this approach were numerous, and it was not impossible to hear one's wealth or position claimed as evidence of one's righteousness before God. (We may still act as if that were true.) But in a more authentic way, the notion that one's station in life (one's job, family, and citizenship—all one's opportunities and duties) was the place where one was to serve God and live out one's Christian faith was a fruitful idea. It meant and still means that in every moment and not only while praying or worshiping or witnessing we are serving God and are in relation to him. It meant and still means that what we do in our "secular" life is important and makes a difference—not to our salvation but to the continuation and even the improvement of God's world.

Vocation and Law

The fact that this understanding of vocation diminished as the idea of God became less important, so that we now tend to think of the world as merely secular and autonomous and to think of a vocation as only an occupation, need not mean that the idea of vocation is no longer useful. It is important to rejuvenate the Reformation idea of vocation if we are to be able to do justice to the biblical notions of creation and redemption and if we are going to provide concrete ways for faith to be lived out responsibly in the world.

If our vocation as Christians is lived out in the world it will be lived according to the *law*, since the law expresses God's will in the created world. It is not that we will live unaffected by the gospel, for it is the gospel that allows us to see our various tasks, responsibilities, and opportunities as callings from God. But the law, with its prohibitions and guidelines and punishments, will be operative in our vocations. And in the area of the law, reason is the ruling factor (along with facts, planning, and plain hard work). Not love, not forgiveness, not hope, but reason. This does not mean that Christians will not love or forgive or hope while doing their work in the world, but that they will realize that the world is under the rule of sin and death, and therefore reason and realism will be called for. At the same time, the gospel reveals that the purpose of the law is love for the neighbor, and so Christians in their vocations will always keep that purpose in mind and will not sink merely to whatever will work or whatever they can get by with.

A second area that needs to be brought up here is related to our salvation and to the "second use" of the law. To use shorthand, law and gospel are not only concerned with our justification but also with our sanctification. "Sanctification" in popular understanding has usually been understood as progress toward greater holiness. But we have seen that there are serious problems with such thinking. Our idea of vocation can help to shape a better understanding of sanctification.

If, even though forgiven and declared righteous ("justified"), we remain in this life totally sinful, then this sinful self (or the "old Adam", as Luther called it) needs to be put to death. Properly understood, this is sanctification—the putting to death of the sinful self so that only the self which is righteous in Christ remains. God puts us to death by the law (second use) which accuses, convicts, crushes, and kills— and then by his grace alone, on the last day, will raise us up with Christ. This "being put to death by the law" or "daily dying" (Luther) is not only a metaphorical way of speaking— as many have thought, equating dying daily with repenting— but it also and primarily refers to our actual death.

According to this way of thinking, our vocation is precisely where we live under the law, and therefore our vocation also will be the place where God puts us to death. God kills the "old Adam" through our laboring by the sweat of our brow and through our being forced to work and serve our families and our society.

This negative and grim-sounding view of vocation has not always been noticed by those who propound the "Protestant ethic." Often we have spoken only in much more positive ways of our callings, which has led to the common idea that, for the Christian, life and work should always be "meaningful." While there is some truth in this, and many of us love our vocations, it misses the fact of God's judgment on us which will be worked out at the same time through our vocations.

To put it another way, "in Christ" we ought to be glad to die (as Paul was when he wrote Phil. 1:23), but "in Adam" we fear death, and so God "helps" us die daily—not primarily through religious rituals and practices but primarily through our vocations (remember that "vocation" is being used here to include work, family, and everything in our situation). The *creative purpose* of vocation is to help us to serve God and keep his world going; but the *redemptive purpose* of our vocation is to discipline us, and that is the same purpose which the law has in its second use.

Vocation and Gospel

The full story of our vocation cannot be be told without relating it more fully to the gospel, however. We have said that the gospel of our justification by faith on account of Christ frees us from ourselves for our neighbors, from the law for the law, and from seeing our jobs as merely drudgery to vocation. Notice, then, that while the gospel urges us to love our neighbors, that is the same thing which the law intends. In that we are wholly new creatures, the gospel and the freedom it gives is sufficient. Faith leaps into good works; it is active in love. Faith does willingly and spontaneously what the law requires. But since we are simultaneously old and new, our old self needs the demands of the law.

The intriguing thing here is that while the law is putting us to death through its demands in our vocation, *at the same time*, precisely in our vocation, the new self is exercising faith by loving the neighbor through vocation. The gospel proclaims the importance of vocation. Without the gospel, our responsibilities would not be vocation but only condemnation (no matter how profitable or stimulating—for we would still have to retire and die). But without vocation, the gospel would be cheap grace—resurrection without crucifixion.

Therefore it is profoundly true to say that vocation is the way of life with a cross at its center. When Christ talked about our being his disciples, he did not say that we are to take up *his* cross; rather, we are to take up *our own* cross. Our cross is the instrument of our death. It will be laid on us by our vocation; we do not seek it or choose it. Our vocation makes it real for us; and thus our sanctification is hidden in ordinary tasks. In the demands and sufferings of our callings we are crucified with Christ. This both serves God's creative purposes, in that our vocation enables and compels us to love and help others, and at the same time accomplishes our salvation by putting to death the sinful self. The love that arises from faith does what vocation demands. Love is law only for the old self, not for the new self.

This hidden and often baffling work of giving life by putting to death, of bringing life out of death and nothingness, is the work of God's Spirit. Nearly all of what the Bible says about God's Spirit has to do with *creating life*—whether that is in Genesis 1:2 or 2:7 (translated "breath") or in Psalm 104:29-30 or in Job 33:4 or Ezekiel 37:9 or in 1 Corinthians 15:45 or in the four gospels' depiction of Jesus as healing and forgiving sins in the power of the Spirit. The Spirit is sent to do the work of creating new life by joining us to Christ, who is the "new Adam", the "first-fruits" of the new creation. The Spirit does this by bringing us into Christ, by joining us to him, so that what happened to Christ happens now to us.

We have already spoken of how this is worked out on a practical level in our vocation. Next we shall talk more explicitly about the Spirit joining us to Christ by baptism.

For further reading:

Forell, George—*Faith Active in Love*
Heiges, Donald—*The Christian's Calling*
Wingren, Gustaf—*Luther on Vocation*

QUESTIONS FOR DISCUSSION

1. Do you think it is true to the Bible to consider worldly actions to be as important as religious practices, as the author asserts?

2. What do you think of the idea that our vocation is the place where God simultaneously allows and compels us to serve him *and* puts us to death?

3. Vocation without the gospel is condemnation. The gospel without vocation is cheap grace. What do you understand this to mean?

8 · Baptism into Christ

Do you not know that all of us who have been baptized into Christ Jesus were baptized into his death? We were buried therefore with him by baptism into death, so that as Christ was raised from the dead by the glory of the Father, we too might walk in newness of life.

For if we have been united with him in a death like his, we shall certainly be united with him in a resurrection like his. We know that our old self was crucified with him so that the sinful body might be destroyed, and we might no longer be enslaved to sin. For he who has died is freed from sin. But if we have died with Christ, we believe that we shall also live with him.

—ROMANS 6:3-8

Perhaps there should be a sign attached to every baptismal font, saying: "Warning: Baptism has been determined to be hazardous to your health."

60

How could that be? A little water applied to your head—hazardous to your health? It is surely not going to drown you! But wait—did all these things happen to you?

- Do you renounce the devil and all his works and all his ways?
- Receive the sign of the holy cross, in token that henceforth thou shalt know the Lord, and the power of his resurrection, and the fellowship of his sufferings.
- Grant that this child now to be baptized may ever remain in the number of the faithful and elect children.
- Keep her in this grace that she may never depart from thee but may always live according to thy will.
- God, the Father of our Lord Jesus Christ, we give you thanks for freeing your sons and daughters from the power of sin and for raising them up to a new life through this holy sacrament.

Did all that happen to you? That's hazardous to your health! That's positively lethal! You are never going to recover; you are not going to live the "good life;" you are not going to be able to grab all the gusto; you are not going to be a "success"—because you have been baptized.

Jesus' Baptism

Ordinarily, when we think of baptism we probably picture a family with a beautifully dressed little baby up in front of a church, with a minister in long robes pouring handfuls of water on the baby's head. It is a happy occasion—and there is surely no feeling that it is hazardous to the baby's health.

To get at what I mean by this, let us begin with Jesus' own

baptism. All four gospels report his baptism by John in the Jordan River. Jesus' baptism was unique in that, unlike other baptisms, he was not baptized for the forgiveness of sins; rather, in his baptism he was anointed with God's Spirit and proclaimed to be the Son of God. Yet even in these aspects of his baptism, there are parallels with our own baptisms— for we say that in baptism God gives us his Spirit and makes us his children.

What is more significant about Jesus' baptism than simply what happened at that moment in time is the way in which baptism continued in his life. The Spirit who came to him in baptism immediately led him into the wilderness to be tempted. And the tempter began by calling into question Jesus' baptism: "*If* you are the Son of God . . . ." Then, in the Gospel of Luke, after beginning his ministry of healing and teaching, Jesus returns to his hometown of Nazareth announcing that God's Spirit is upon him because God has anointed him to preach a radical message of good news to the poor, release to the captives, sight to the blind, liberty to the oppressed, and the cancellation of all debts (the "acceptable year of the Lord", in Luke 4:19, apparently is a reference to the Jewish year of Jubilee, when some sort of economic justice was to be reestablished).

After initially being impressed by Jesus, people soon got the point that he was speaking about their own sinfulness and the injustice which they perpetrated and tolerated. Jesus brought judgment, he caused discomfort, he raised embarrassing questions. And this all followed from his baptism, when he was named God's Son and given God's Spirit. But this was not the sort of "anointed one" (in Hebrew, "Messiah") the people had been expecting. This was not a warrior king who would set his people up in a glorious kingdom on earth; this was a leader who sided with the poor and the outcasts, who got into trouble and caused trouble, and who was heading for a fall.

Even his own disciples were disturbed by Jesus' behavior and teachings. When Jesus asked them what they thought about him, Peter spoke for them all and confessed that Jesus was indeed the "Christ" (the Greek word for Messiah or "anointed one"—see Matt. 16, Mark 8, and Luke 9). But Jesus immediately went on to define what was entailed in his being designated as Christ. He told them that he must suffer many things, and be rejected, and be killed, and on the third day be raised from the dead. The disciples couldn't accept this. Peter said, "God forbid, Lord! This shall never happen to you." (He was probably thinking, "God forbid, Lord! This must never happen to *me*—but if I'm your follower and it happens to you—no, it must never happen to you.")

The point for us is that Jesus' baptism was the beginning of a life and ministry that headed toward the cross. And lest you think that baptism really couldn't have included all of that, hear what Jesus says about his own baptism. He speaks about it in only two places, Luke 12:50 and Mark 10:35-40. In Luke 12, nine chapters after he was first baptized in the Jordan by John, Jesus says: "I have a baptism *to be* baptized with; and how I am constrained *until* it is accomplished!" What is he talking about?

In Mark 10, Jesus told his disciples for the third time that he will be tortured and killed. But two of them, apparently not having understood a thing, ask for a little glory for themselves. To which Jesus replies: "You do not know what you are asking. Are you able . . . to be baptized with the baptism

with which I *am* baptized?" Then he adds ruefully that they
will be, all right.

Now, to what is Jesus referring when he speaks about his
baptism in this way—in neither case in the past tense but
in one case as a future event and in the second case as a
present happening? He is speaking about his suffering and
crucifixion. *His death is his baptism.*

Remember—in those days there were no church buildings,
no formal baptismal services, no sacraments, and no ministers
in long robes. Baptism was not only a religious word, but a
word which meant washing, bathing, immersing, drowning,
and even refers to the sinking of a ship. Thus when Jesus
says that he has a "baptism to be baptized with" he means
that he must go through something, he must be "immersed"
in something. Baptism, first of all, is an action word.

We sometimes still use "baptism" as an action word. In
the final months of World War II, when the United States
was drafting all sorts of men who had previously been declared too old or too young or in too poor health, the train-
ing camps were woefully overcrowded and undersupplied.
So it happened that men would go to the front lines never
having trained with live gunfire and never having shot the
type of rifles they were issued at the front. When they got
into their first battle it was a real battle against the enemy,
and they were said to have gotten their "baptism by fire."
Jesus speaks of his baptism in the same way—as something
he must go through.

Our Baptism

If we see clearly that Jesus' baptism refers above all to his
death, then we will have a better basis for making sense of
our own baptism. In the New Testament "being baptized"

comes to be a parallel expression for "being crucified with Christ." (See, for example, 1 Cor. 1:13—"Was Paul crucified for you? Or were you baptized in the name of Paul?") This insight has helped me to make sense of several other passages which I knew were important but from which I could not get any meaning. In Romans 6:3, Paul writes, "Do you not know that all of us who have been baptized with Christ were baptized into his *death?*" This starts to make sense when I link it to Jesus' own baptism—now understood as his whole life-and-ministry-unto-death. Then we might read Paul's statement to mean that "all of us who have been immersed with Christ have been immersed into his whole life-and-ministry-unto-death."

Other words also begin to make sense, as when in Romans 6:4 Paul goes on to say: "We were buried therefore with him by baptism into death, so that as Christ was raised from the dead by the glory of the father, we too might walk in newness of life." Our being baptized means our participation with Christ in his still ongoing ministry, his mission, his causes, his calling, his works, his *dying*, and (finally) his resurrection.

This is what was meant by the statement that baptism is hazardous to your health. It means that you lose your life to live Christ's life. There are some similarities to being drafted for military service. You cannot get out of it. You can be a deserter, but you are still a member of the armed forces. You are no longer free to come and go as you please. You live now for your nation.

Put in such terms, baptism may sound like a bad thing. If that is so, why would anyone be baptized, or why would we have our babies baptized? It sounds as if when you are baptized, you lose your freedom—you don't get to live any longer for yourself because now you have to live for Christ. The illusion here, of course, is that doing what we please is freedom. Baptism is hazardous to the illusion that we are free; it is hazardous to the health which we delude ourselves that we possess.

In reality, as we noted in previous chapters, we are not free. We are in bondage to death and to our own self-centeredness and to all the other bondages these drive us into. Therefore, when we are baptized, when we get involved with Christ's ongoing life-and-ministry-unto death, this is not a loss of freedom—for we didn't have any real freedom to lose! Being set free isn't being cut loose. Freedom as Christianity understands it is more like the experience of one who was a citizen of a country in which no freedom is allowed, and who was then rescued from that country to become a citizen of a nation which allows a person to live freely. The person will now have many more responsibilities and duties as an active participant in society, but this will joyfully be called "freedom." Freedom is a positive thing: freedom *from* something (bondage) and freedom *for* something.

Jesus said, "Whoever would save his life will lose it; and whoever loses his life for my sake . . . will save it" (Mark 8:35). When you were baptized into Christ, you began to lose your life . . . and find it.

For further reading:

Cullmann, Oscar—*Baptism in the New Testament*
Jungkuntz, Richard—*The Gospel of Baptism*
Marty, Martin—*Baptism*
Wingren, Gustaf—*Gospel and Church*, Part I

QUESTIONS FOR DISCUSSION

1. "Baptism is not an eternal life insurance policy." What do you think of such a statement?
2. Who is the *actor* in baptism?
3. Reread the passage from Romans 6 at the beginning of this chapter. Does it make more sense if we think of Jesus' own baptism as his death?

9 · Baptism into Christ's Body

*For just as the body is one and has many mem-
bers, and all the members of the body, though
many, are one body, so it is with Christ. For by
one Spirit we were all baptized into one body—
Jews or Greeks, slaves or free—and all were
made to drink of one Spirit.*

—1 Corinthians 12:12-13

The way in which Jesus spoke of his own baptism pointed
ahead to his death. His baptism was something which began
his life's vocation and continued through his crucifixion. So
also with our baptism. When the water is poured on and
the words are spoken, we are given our life's vocations as
members of God's family. And this goes on and on until our
death. This is true even if we don't feel it, even if we rebel
against it; we have been baptized and that doesn't stop.

It is not unlike being born into a family. You may not
always like your parents and brothers and sisters, you may

68

leave home, you may say that you don't want anything to do with your family any more. But the fact is that you are a member of that family whether you like it or not. And finally, for most of us, this is a real blessing. As the old saying puts it, "Home is where, when you have to go there, they have to take you in."

Perhaps it seems a bit strange to regard baptism that way, but it does take seriously our own sinfulness, recalcitrance, and self-centeredness. God's family is where, when we finally realize that we need to go there, they have to take us in— because we have been baptized into Christ, and God's family, the church, is Christ's very own body.

By illustrating baptism in this way, I do not want to give the impression that it is some sort of inevitable eternal life insurance policy. The fact that baptism is seen as a life-long vocation should guard against such a misunderstanding— though it surely won't for those who see baptism as a mere formality gone through to please Grandma! But I do want to make the point that baptism is God's doing. When we are baptized *God* is acting through his word and his creation—*giving* us his Spirit, giving us forgiveness of sins, new life, and salvation by *calling* us to be members of his family, adopted brothers and sisters of his Son, Jesus Christ. (And as Paul wrote about another stubborn group of God's people, "The gifts and the call of God are irrevocable"— Rom. 11:29.) Baptism does not depend on how we feel or on what we do. Rather, it is to give shape to what we feel and do from here on out.

You Can't Be a Christian Alone

Because of this understanding of baptism, to be a Christian does *not* mean to have Jesus in your heart, it does *not* mean possessing the Holy Spirit, and it does *not* mean accepting Christ as your personal savior. To be a Christian *does* mean being a member of Christ's body, but not *my* possessing him in *my* heart. It *does* mean being present in the sphere of the Holy Spirit's work, but who could have the Spirit of *God* as his or her own personal possession? It *does* mean trusting that *Christ* accepts me, but not the other way around, lest my own act of acceptance become the foundation on which my religion is built.

The phrases at the beginning of the previous paragraph, which I rejected even though they are commonly used by Christians, were rejected because they are evidence of the continued existence of the sinful self, the "old Adam." The old Adam seeks to set the terms for his relationship with God; he wants to have God *and* his old, sinful self—but God says that the sinful self must die. The old Adam wants to make his religion a private and self-centered affair—but when God makes us his children we find that we have many brothers and sisters.

If to be a Christian is really summed up in baptism—being united with Christ's death and resurrection to participate with him from here to eternity in his ongoing work—then we will find ourselves in the church, Christ's body. That may be offensive to many of us, since Christian individualism is a dearly loved American contribution to the history of heresy. But then the Bible was not written by Americans!

This notion that one has to be in the church to be a Christian is offensive to many people for several reasons. It is said that "You can pick your friends but not your relatives." And just as I want to pick my friends, I want to pick my fellow-Christians. But we were all baptized into the one body of Christ—Jews and Greeks, slaves and free, blacks and Hispanics, Laotians and Native Americans, rich and poor, Republicans and Democrats—and all are now our relatives in Christ. Yet many people who are different from me make me uncomfortable.

This was a problem even in Jesus' time. "Riffraff" and "undesirables" hung around with Jesus. However, it soon became clear with whom Jesus sided. The meaning for us is that we cannot have Christ without having our neighbor. If we reject our neighbor, we reject Christ; and our neighbor is anyone in need. Think of the words in the parable of the sheep and the goats in Matthew 25: "As you did it to one of the least of these my brethren, you did it to me." Christianity is not a private affair. It is intensely personal, but not private, for it is being "in Christ," in his body, and that body has many members.

So what do we do? Do we grin and bear it like the wealthy white country club members who now have to let in the rich blacks? Hardly! It is not as if other people are something we have to put up with if we want to get to heaven. That is the old Adam's way of thinking. Being in the church with all Christ's other people is for our own good. In his wisdom God gives us other people so that we will be pulled outside of ourselves, because being turned in on ourselves is what sin is all about. These other people themselves are part of our salvation! We meet Christ in them; we are to be Christ to them. God's Spirit works through external means, as the Reformers said—through words and water, bread and wine, and other people. Thank God, we cannot be Christians alone.

Baptism and the Church

Another reason why we are offended by the claim that to be a Christian means to be part of the church is that the reality of the church doesn't seem to live up to its claims or our expectations. When we see a congregation up close, with all its shortcomings and pettiness, with all the hypocrites who belong, and with all the evidence of the old Adam at work in every area and in every decision, we really have trouble seeing how this is a place in which we are to live out the fact that we have been baptized.

Part of the problem is with the church itself. If it is an organization it will be made up of persons, and at best each of these will be *simul iustus et peccator* (at the same time righteous and sinful). If we remember that we are speaking of the righteousness which is known by faith, that is, forgiveness, then we will be warned not to expect perfection. Sin is present in every person and it is compounded when persons become grouped in organizations. That is why one thing that needs to be said is that "the church always needs to be reformed." We will think about the nature and mission of the church along these lines in the next chapter.

Part of the problem we have with the church, however, is *our* problem. This problem is related to the sort of "arms' length" approach we often take to our relationship with God. We think that God is "out there" and we are here and we are supposed to believe in him or please him or whatever. Against such a view, by speaking of being a Christian as our participation in Christ's ongoing work, I have been trying to counter our tendency to separate ourselves and God. I have been trying to overcome the almost mechanical way we often think about our faith. Note that I did not say that our faith is mechanical. I believe that few people are unaware of at least some relationship to the one who is their origin and destiny in a way that is hardly mechanical. But sometimes we *think* about our faith mechanically.

For example, it is often said that baptism is our entrance into the church. This is often taken to mean that it is the process or event of joining an organization—which is often quite mechanical. Churches themselves have often been most at fault here—identifying actual organizations and structures with the body of Christ. This is easy enough to account for, since those of us who speak most often about the church tend to be employed by church organizations and preoccupied with "church business," but it is quite misleading.

It is all right to say that baptism is our entrance or initiation into the church if we understand that the church is not primarily a human organizaion but is the "people of God" or the "body of Christ" or the "sphere of the Spirit's work." These titles transcend and transform any given religious organization, though not in such a way that we do not need particular religious organizations.

What Is the Church?

Much thought was given to the question "What is the church?" during the sixteenth century Reformation, largely because the Protestants had to give reasons why their groups could rightfully be called churches. Lutherans said that the church is "the assembly of believers among whom the gospel is preached in its purity (that is, proclaiming that we are justified by faith) and the sacraments are administered in accordance with the Gospel." The Calvinists said nearly the same thing, adding a clause about Christian people living lives of discipleship. The point is that the church was defined in terms of the message of God's saving actions (Word and sacraments) being received by people in faith. Today, Roman Catholics also have begun to stress images of the church which focus on God's action among his people rather than on institutional forms as constituting the essence of the church. It becomes apparent that it is important for our personal life of faith that we think and speak carefully about the church.

Since the church tends to come to mean buildings and religious organizations and professional ministers just because these are what we bump into, I want to spell out some added implications which follow from the definition of the church being advocated here. The Swedish theologian Gustaf Wingren has said, "Men and women in their places of work are the church." Perhaps this overstates the case, but let us look at it. *If* we say that baptism means that we are Christ's, that we are reborn, and that we are brought into the family of God; and *if* God is the one who creates anew perpetually and who wills for us to be his creatures; and *if* the Holy Spirit who is given in baptism is the same Spirit who is the creative agent of God; *then* our being baptized by the Spirit into the church will have to do primarily with our lives in our "places of work" (this being a shorthand phrase for all aspects of our vocations). The church is God's people in their callings, and the assembled congregation is just one aspect of what "church" actually includes.

This is a large claim, so let us follow it step by step. In the beginning God said, "Let us make humans in our own image." However, because of sin, none of us is in the image of God. That is why the New Testament calls Jesus alone the image of God (Col. 1:15): Jesus was the first person in whom God's image was realized. Thus, when we are joined to Christ in baptism it is for the purpose of bringing about in us, finally, the image of God. In baptism God's creative Spirit is still at work, *completing creation* by creating faith and sending people out as creatures in vocations. Thus men and women in their places of work are the church.

Talking in this way would be clear enough except that today many people are confused about the work of the Holy Spirit. There is much loose and unscriptural talk to the effect that the primary gift of the Holy Spirit is "speaking in tongues," or that if we "have" the Spirit supernatural things will happen or we will hear private revelations from God. But think a moment. The work of the Holy Spirit is to create in us faith in Christ so as to bring about in us the image of God. But the image of God is not concerned with speaking in tongues or with the supernatural. The image of God is *Jesus Christ*. His shape is to take place in us. And what is his shape? Suffering, death, and resurrection! Giving and forgiving! The Holy Spirit is given to us in baptism to bring about our death, and then our resurrection.

Our death and resurrection is worked out in us by the Spirit through our vocations—not through special "spiritual" experiences, not through anything supernatural at all, but through the natural creaturely life of "men and women in their places of work." Of course, none of this emphasis on the worldliness of our life of faith is meant to deny the vital importance of gathering for worship and study and other involvement in Christian congregations. But it is meant to emphasize that the church exists *for* the world and not the other way around. It is through the preaching and teaching of the law and the gospel and the administration of the sacraments that the Spirit will be able to do his work in us through our vocations.

All of this was implied, I think, in the Reformation view of the church because back then virtually every citizen was also a member of the church and assembled for worship each Sunday. Therefore the Christian message reached into every aspect of daily life, into every vocation, and it could hardly be thought that the church was a private club for the religiously inclined. Since the situation has changed in our day, we need to renew our understanding of the church not primarily in terms of current thinking about social groups or institutional growth, nor in terms of the dynamics of interpersonal relationships, but in terms of our understanding of the meaning of the Christian message.

For further reading:
   Bonhoeffer, Dietrich—*Life Together*
   Wingren, Gustaf—*Gospel and Church*, Part II

QUESTIONS FOR DISCUSSION

1. Do you agree that you can't be a Christian alone?
2. What do you think of the idea that God's salvation involves us with other people as a means of keeping us from self-centeredness?
3. What do you see as strengths and weaknesses of the Reformation definitions of the church?
4. Discuss the idea that the church is Christian people in their callings.

10 · The Church

*A seven-year-old child knows what the church is,
namely, holy believers and sheep who hear the
voice of their Shepherd.*

—MARTIN LUTHER

There are two common ways of thinking about the church.
Roman Catholics, at least until the Second Vatican Council
(1962-65), have usually understood the church in *institutional* and *hierarchical* terms. "Hierarchical" here means being
ruled by properly constituted bishops and priests, *hieros* being
the Greek word for priest. Against this, most Protestants have
argued for a view of the church which verges on seeing it as
occasional. "Occasional" refers to seeing the church as existing only on those occasions when the Word is being preached
or taught, or the sacraments are being administered to the
assembled faithful, or Christians are engaged in mission. In
this view, the organization we normally call the church is not
the church in its proper sense.

Both views have some obvious values. The institutional view takes God's incarnation very seriously. It sees that the reality of God's work now takes place as it did in Christ— that is, in and through earthly forms and practices. By identifying Christ's body with a certain organization, it makes clear to people how they are to be united with Christ. And, in the hostile times in which this view first arose in the early church, joining a Christian institution was clearly an act of faith which changed one's whole life; this is still the case in some countries with totalitarian governments.

The value of the second view is that it distinguishes clearly between the Creator and the creation and between the divine and the human. It says that no organization can be identified through and through with God's presence or his work. It seeks to keep the church from becoming an end in itself or an idol. Rather, it stresses that the reality of faith is a hidden thing, which transcends membership in any earthly group.

Both views also have their weaknesses. The hierarchical church can easily become a corrupt and oppressive institution, serving the status quo and the powers that be and obscuring the God whom it claims to represent. The occasional view, on the other hand, easily fades into seeing the church merely as a gathering of like-minded people with a stress on individual spiritual experience, which often moves toward legalism, moralism, and quietism. Neither view does justice to the reality many of us know as "church"—a reality that transcends its fallible members, leaders, and structures, and a reality that continues even when the preaching and sacraments are not happening.

The Apostles' and Nicene Creeds are probably wiser when they speak first about the Holy Spirit and then include a phrase about the church. For the church is a creation of the

Spirit. In Luther's words, the Holy Spirit "calls, gathers, enlightens, sanctifies, and preserves" the Christian church. The Spirit does this by bearing witness to Christ and drawing people to him (John 14-17, 1 Cor. 12). In all of our thinking about the church we need to remember that the gospel concerning Christ comes first—and the church follows from that.

How Shall the Church Be Defined?

As the proliferation of denominations attests, Christians have a great deal of trouble agreeing about the church. Denominational labels aside, there is a type of Christian position which would say that while the hierarchical view alone is not adequate, it does get at a most important characteristic of the church, namely, *continuity*. It hangs on to continuity with the original leaders of the church and their episcopal structure ("episcopal" is from the Greek word for "bishop"). Or it may retain continuity with the teaching of the apostles or with the forms and practices of the church through the ages. The point is, they say, that the true church is to be found in continuity with what has come to be through the centuries.

This type is not limited to Roman Catholics; at the very least, it would include also the Eastern Orthodox, the Anglicans, and many Lutherans, especially in European state churches. The emphases in this type are on the close relationship of the church to its surrounding society, on its cultural role of nourishing and educating large numbers of people, and on its influence as an ancient and well-established force in its society. There is strength and stability in this type of church. It is usually led by trained clergy, and it is supported by buildings, social welfare systems, music, public acceptance, and the opportunity to play a key role in the important events

of people's lives (birth, puberty, marriage, illness, and death)
as well as in national observances (holidays, centennials, coro-
nations, tragedies, and the like).

The weaknesses of any hierarchical institution tend to apply
to this type of church (for example, stagnation, corruption,
loss of real purpose), but there are other problems with this
view as well. It has to show or justify how everything that
exists now is in continuity with the past, and thus it is not
able to deal with the newness of God's creative work. Even
worse, it is often tied to a fictitious past—for example, claiming that Peter was the first pope, even though there is no
historical evidence for this; or claiming that earlier doctrines
or worship forms were the same as something which we are
thinking or doing now, even though there is no way in which
the ancient period can be thought of as being identical with
the modern world.

It is no wonder that all through history there have been
Christians who have rejected this understanding of the church.
Over and over "sectarian" (separatist) groups have sought
instead to *restore* the pure church of the New Testament
period in place of the corrupt entity which, they say, the existing church has become. Such reform movements have had a
clear sense of the difference between God's truth and his ways
and our sinful ways. They have stressed the need for individual conversion and not only for belonging to an institution;
they have called for purity of life in contrast to the evils of
society. They have been suspicious of professional ministers
with their tendency to supersede the freedom of the Spirit's
work by controlling church structures and the sacraments.
These sectarian restorationists have recaptured the sense of
urgency which the New Testament has concerning the im-

pending judgment and the second coming of Christ—a sense which lessens the importance of all existing institutions.

Some clear values of this position have been its critical strength (using a biblical view of the church as an ideal by which to criticize the present church) and its emphasis on personal commitment rather than organizational membership. This in turn has led to a stress on the importance of *all* the people of God (the laity, from *laos,* meaning "people") as well as on the study of the Bible. Most Protestants, including many Lutherans, would find this type of understanding of the church quite congenial.

Yet for all its strengths, the weaknesses of this approach are great. For one thing, there is no single dominant view of the church in the New Testament. The many present-day groups, all claiming to be *the* biblical form of the church, make this clear to us and underscore the results of modern New Testament study. Indeed, the amazing thing we now know about the early church is its astonishing multiplicity of forms, practices, and teachings. Thus the restoration approach also must be tied to a fictitious past. Worse, it claims to ignore nineteen hundred years of history and tradition in basing its understanding only on the Bible. This is uncritical as well as impossible. Yet it means that Christians who think this way will not be able explicitly to take into account the new insights of the present and future or to see God acting creatively there either.

Evangelical Pragmatism

A way beyond these impasses may be found in the experiences and writings of Martin Luther and John Wesley. Neither of these men, who are remembered for changing the church, set out to reform the church or to give a new definition of it. Rather, they were overwhelmed by discovering a new view of God as forgiving, merciful, loving, and justifying. That *message* was the basis for everything else they did. And each can best be understood, when it comes to their teachings about the church, as an "evangelical pragmatist." "Evangelical," it will be remembered, refers to the gospel or the good news. Thus, "evangelical pragmatism" means that whatever forms and practices serve the gospel can and should be used. This is a pragmatism (that is, doing what works best) in the service of the message of the gospel.

In the sixteenth century, Luther, unlike many of the other Reformers, retained many of the Roman Catholic Church's practices as long as they did not hinder faith even if they could not be found in the Bible. Yet he was equally quick to discard things in the name of the gospel—if they were obstructions to faith, such as the use of Latin. In principle this meant that even practices and forms from the Bible could be rejected if they proved to be a hindrance to faith at a later time (for example: slavery, sexism). This is evangelical pragmatism.

So also Wesley in the eighteenth century began to spread the gospel in dramatic new ways even while considering himself to be a loyal priest of the Church of England. Yet because his criterion for action was now different (that is, do whatever serves the gospel), new actions were possible, such as evangelizing in the fields, while old actions, such as ordaining pastors, might be retained but now for different reasons.

This evangelical pragmatism is potentially a tremendous asset for us in thinking about the church because it is so *flexible*. It should mean that we are not tied to a single form of church or ministry. It should certainly not demand uniformity as a condition for church unity. Shaping the forms and practices of the church in the years to come along these lines would mean that we would be open to new information and insights from whatever sources. This view is also *responsible:* it does not simply accept what has come to be as what must continue forever, but it begins anew in each generation by rethinking and reforming in accord with the message of the gospel.

There are potential dangers here too, of course. Because no particular forms are required (in terms of ministry, worship, governance, and Christian living), this approach may not pay sufficient attention to the forms we already have. They may need to go, but, on the other hand, they may be more valuable than we have realized. At times our forms have actually undercut the gospel. Often the church has simply reflected the dominant forms of its surrounding society, so that in America our churches are run basically as small businesses and in Europe they look like government agencies. This drastically diminishes our ability to speak prophetic (critical) words to our society, among other problems.

The tendency for forms and practices that were once established pragmatically, and once served the gospel well, to be retained long after they have ceased to be functional is probably a worse danger. Examples here could run from the trivial, such as the time for worship and the use of candles, to more substantive issues, such as the sex and role of pastors or the notion of the geographical parish.

The worst danger of evangelical pragmatism as a way of thinking about the church is that "evangelical" may drop out and "pragmatism" alone may remain, so that whatever works is thought to be good. Then any technique that gets more members, no matter how manipulative, or any program that raises money, no matter how legalistic, can be used—even if it undercuts or contradicts the gospel of God's free grace.

Being aware of these dangers can help us use this approach more effectively. We ought to stress that evangelical pragmatism is not a way of thinking that calls on us to discard everything we previously had. It is correct to speak of Martin Luther, for example, as a conserving if not a conservative Reformer. Many more radical forms of Protestantism, on the other hand, have been impoverished by the rejection of what the theologian Paul Tillich called "Catholic substance." A truly evangelical pragmatism will realize the values of some traditional forms and practices, but it will retain what it retains for the proper reasons. Just because something is ancient does not make it either good or bad, although I would be a bit cautious in this regard and give what has been done before the benefit of the doubt—other things being equal. In other words, this position does not advocate change simply for the sake of change.

Because of its awareness of the radicality of sin, Lutheran theology has been wise here in insisting that order, even unjust or inefficient order, is preferable to chaos. But it has often been guilty of judging every movement for change to be chaos! In other words, an evangelical pragmatist ought to value tradition without being a traditional*ist*. (Someone has said that "tradition is the living faith of dead people; tradition*ism* is the dead faith of living people.") The content of the Christian tradition has at its center the God who does new things and who gives us radical freedom. What we conserve, therefore, is dynamic and we dare not seek to domesticate it.

The message of the gospel is the most important thing about the church. Any particular forms of church or ministry are to be established, continued, or altered primarily in terms of whether they serve the proclamation of the gospel and the mission of those who believe this gospel. Our primary loyalty is to Christ, after all, and not to human organizations.

For further reading:

Dulles, Avery—*Models of the Church*
Neuhaus, Richard John—*Freedom for Ministry*
Paul, Robert S.—*The Church in Search of Its Self*
Schwarz, Hans—*The Christian Church*

QUESTIONS FOR DISCUSSION

1. How do you usually define the church? How would your definition relate to the various types mentioned in this chapter?

2. If, for some reason, you could not belong to a congregation of your denomination, to what denomination would you probably belong? Why? (Answering this question will help you to identify what things about the church are most important to you.)

3. An old saying puts it: "Outside the church there is no salvation." A modern sociologist has observed that this saying makes good sense in sociological terms, because outside the church faith tends to die from lack of social reinforcement. What do you think about this?

11 · The Church's Mission

The vocation of the church is to sustain many vocations.

—RICHARD JOHN NEUHAUS

Two Alternative Views

Given the understanding of the Christian message outlined in previous chapters, and given the preceding ideas about what the church is, how might we think about its mission or purpose?

Perhaps the predominant view which we have inherited says that God does his work primarily through the church, and the church has a mission for the world. This is familiar to most Christians. The main question is, "How do we reach those who do not yet believe with our gospel?" The goal of our efforts will be to bring people into the fellowship of the church because it is the place where God is present in a meaningful and saving way. In addition, because we in the church have been given many gifts by God, we are to bring them to the rest of the world by doing works of love, reconciliation, and healing.

The activities which will be important for the Christian are governed by the assumptions lying behind this view. Corporate worship is important because God is thought to be present there in ways in which he is not present in the world, where he is hidden and his ways are ambiguous. Witness is important because without the church's telling people about salvation in Christ, no one would be able to know him or serve him. The "care of souls" (to use an old phrase) is stressed because the important activities in our Christian life center on our personal relationship to God: confession and repentance, prayer, study, and fellowship with other Christians. Pastors or priests have a key role in this work, because they bring the word of grace and the sacraments. Finally, this approach stresses the growth in faith of individuals, who then will affect the world through their daily lives (this is the Protestant version), or it stresses the gradual growth by people into involvement with the church, which will then corporately affect its surrounding society (Catholic version). The common denominator here is growth from the inside out (from the church to the world).

Such a view may lead to arrogance and inaction (for example: "we have the truth; if people want it they can come to us"). It may also allow a congregationalism or parochialism which leads to churches becoming clubs for the like-minded. These were among the reasons that called forth an alternative approach during the past few decades. There were theological reasons for this new view as well, the basic one being identified as the *missio Dei* ("mission of God") theme. It claims that the main point of the biblical message concerning the church is that God is at work in the *world* first of all (and not only or primarily in the church). Thus, *God* has a mission in the world: the mission is not the church's. The church's task is to encourage and explain and participate in those things which God is doing in the world. In the 1960s when this view was most popular, many theologians identified God's mission with things such as seeking justice through the civil rights movement, seeking peace through the anti-war movement, and seeking the liberation of the oppressed through revolutionary movements.

The slogan for this approach was the "the world writes the agenda" for what the church is to do. Since God is thought to be at work transforming society in the direction of his purposes, the church is to support these transformations in every way possible—through direct political action and pressure, through involvement with other groups working for the same goals, and by bringing forth biblically-based guidelines for social change.

Some problems with this view are readily apparent. There is the obvious danger of identifying God's will with causes we like (note that the examples in the previous paragraph are all liberal or leftists movements—at another time in history they could just as easily be those of the far right). A related criticism is that this approach is uncritical about its notion of "the world." Is the world fully in God's power, so that any or all changes in it can be identified with God's will? Surely not. The Bible portrays a significant role for the devil or the power of evil in the world, and if that is so, then the world's agendas no doubt will be ambiguous, at best. Also, it is clear from Scripture that the whole world will not be saved—there will be judgment. To be saved, one must be "in Christ." Such themes are neglected in this approach.

Another criticism is that this alternative tends to blur God's creative and saving actions so that it makes the church (unintentionally, perhaps) necessary in *all* of God's work by not defining the church's mission in terms of proclaiming God's salvation. This expansion of the church's purpose is what the Reformers wanted to avoid, and it is ironic that this "mission of God" position began in opposition to a church-centered point of view. The Bible is quite clear that the church's tasks are related to God's *saving* work: the church is to preach the gospel to all nations. Yet because of this blurring of God's creative and saving work, this alternative approach often neglects the need for Christian nurture or maintenance of the church's own members as well as for Christians to witness to salvation in Christ because of its emphasis on social involvement.

This alternative approach does remind us of several important things, however. It certainly pushes us beyond the narrow parochialism of so much Christianity by insisting that the church exists for the sake of the world. Or, as Luther said, the church exists for the sake of those who are not in it. It also challenges the church not to let society assign it merely "acceptable" roles—-for example, taking care of "marginal" people but not criticizing the system which forces them to the sidelines; or dealing with personal problems and private interests but not challenging social conditions; or helping people cope with problems inflicted by society without seeking to alter society. This position supports evangelical pragmatism by saying that all congregational activities must be for the sake of our larger mission and never only for ourselves. And it strongly stresses the need for Christians to be involved in societal transformation.

A Third View

After becoming fully aware of these two significant ways of thinking about the church's mission, I would like to propose a third way. It would draw on both of the others, but would be organized from a somewhat different point of view. For want of a better term, let us call this the "vocation model" of the church's mission.

This *vocation model* says that God is at work in both the world and the church, but in different ways. God works as Creator and as Redeemer. These are not separate, because redemption is to fulfill and complete creation, but they are distinguishable. The important point for us is that God calls us to faithful participation in *both* the world and the church. Thus the predominant view is correct in saying that God is at work in the church, but it is wrong if it goes on to imply that God is not at work in the world. And the alternative view is correct in saying that God's most basic work is done in the world, but it is misleading when it does not distinguish his creative work from his redemptive work—especially in terms of our participation in them.

The vocation model says that God is at work in the church through the law (second use) and the gospel in Word and sacraments, calling us to faith in Christ and to love and witness toward our neighbors. And the vocation model also says, just as strongly, that God is at work in the world creating and preserving us and all things, and calling us to act in accordance with his will (the first use of the law) within the various legitimate institutions and movements of society (and not only through the church).

According to the vocation model, the Christian's life will have two necessary emphases: church and world. The *church* exists for our salvation, and if salvation is by faith, and if faith comes by hearing (as Rom. 10:17 says), then we must hear the Word regularly. We must hear it in preaching and the sacraments (Luther calls them "visible words"), in study and discussion, and we need to pray for and plan for the life of the congregation where all this takes place—as well as supporting it with our time and money.

There are several helpful ways of describing the church's mission according to the vocation model. Some have spoken of the rhythm of "gathering" and "scattering." Others have spoken of "maintenance" and "mission." Still others have pictured it as "coming" and "going." In any case, the dimension of coming together as an assembly of believers is a necessary part of being maintained in the covenant of baptism, since we must be *crucified* with Christ—we do not go voluntarily to our death—before being raised with him. The gathered and scattered, worshiping and witnessing church is God's means now of doing his redemptive work.

"Evangelism" is a key word here for what we do as participants in God's redemptive work. It means "spreading the good news" about Jesus by our words and deeds. Evangelism is the main corporate task of the church in society, just as it is each Christian's responsibility to tell others about the salvation we have through Christ. Just as surely as we are called together in the church, so also we are sent out as God's messengers into the world.

The vocation model would suggest that we are not sent out only for evangelism or only as church members, however. If that were true it might seem as if the legitimacy of everything we do in the world depends on our connection with a particular Christian institution or rationale. But the *world* has a legitimacy of its own (see Rom. 13), and we are to participate in its structures, movements, organizations, and events as human beings and as creatures, and not only or especially as some sort of specifically religious creatures. Nor will our work in the world be directed only toward certain Christian goals. "Christianizing the social order" or working for "Christian legislation" will not be our purpose. Justice is justice; there is not a special Christian form. There are only Christians and Christian groups who, along with other persons and groups, seek justice.

The reason for distinguishing our tasks as Christians from our tasks as creatures is not that we do not want to make the world a better place to live. Rather, we are aware of the fact that we always remain *simul iustus et peccator* (simultaneously righteous and sinful), and therefore our highest ideals and "purest motives" (even and especially our religious ideals and motives) will be shot through with self-centered aspects. The recent rise of the strident alliance between fundamentalist Christianity and right-wing politics offers still another illustration of the seemingly perpetual interweaving of Christian ideals with sinful self-interest.

That is why we must insist that our service as Christians in the world should be understood as being primarily through our various callings and not through religious involvement in certain secular areas. It would be well if we were as concerned that our members served on the city council as on the church council (and not so that we can get our way with the city council). We should be as appreciative of public school teachers as of Sunday school teachers. We should never allow guilt to be felt by a church member who as a part of his employment with the state government negotiates 16 hours a day with legislative committees in order to wrest additional funds for prisons and mental hospitals, and in the process misses every church building committee meeting for two months.

Yet often we have only paid lip service to Luther's insistence that a scrubwoman doing her job is as important as the preacher or bank president. Really—deep down—don't most of us act as if "full-time Christian service" (to use the old phrase) is somehow better? Yet what would happen to our world (to say nothing of the church) if all Christians went into that sort of full-time service? The content of the whole Christian message, with its robust emphasis on creation, law, and vocation, along with the gospel of salvation through Jesus Christ, needs to be taken much more seriously in shaping our understanding of the church's mission and our participation in it. Vocation, and all that it entails, keeps the church down to earth, and that is where it is meant to be. The church exists on the earth and for the earth, and, in a curious way, *of* the earth—about which we will hear more in the next chapter.

For further reading:
> Diehl, William—*Christianity and Real Life*
> Knutson, Kent S.—*The Shape of the Question*
> Neve, Herbert, ed.—*Sources for Change*
> Weber, H. R.—*Salty Christians*

QUESTIONS FOR DISCUSSION

1. In this chapter a distinction was made between God's *creative* work in the world through its movements and institutions and his *redemptive* work by means of the proclamation of the gospel and the administration of the sacraments through the church and its people. While most of us are aware that we are to be witnesses to our faith in Christ, the

main point of the chapter was to emphasize that our work in God's created order (our society, families, jobs, etc.) is equally as important. Do you agree? Why or why not?

2. Do you think this approach makes specifically Christian tasks, such as church involvement and witnessing, less important?

3. Do you think the vocation model of the church's mission gives you better understanding of how you are related to God in your daily life in "nonreligious" spheres?

4. How would you describe the mission or purpose of the church?

12 · The Lord's Supper

*The means of grace are not ends in themselves,
but means until the end.*

That the church exists on, and for, and of the earth is a
point made most dramatically in the celebration of the Lord's
Supper. There, we who have been baptized into Christ and
his mission are nourished by him on our death walk. The
Lord's Supper is not a feast but a foretaste of things to come—
both crucifixion and resurrection. It is not a banquet, but a
subsistence meal for the journey. It is not a "theophany" (a
dazzling appearance of God in his glory) but a simple mystery in which we are promised that the incarnate God himself
comes to us in the earthly elements of bread and wine.

God's Altar Call

We may wish that God's coming to us were more spiritual
or elevating than this simple meal. Yet by coming to us in

this way God brings us back to earth, back to being creatures, and he forgives us again for the age old sin of pride, whereby we seek to escape our humanness. We might call the Lord's Supper God's "altar call," for here the incarnate Lord himself calls us to his table to receive his crucified body and blood, which were given and shed for us at Calvary for the forgiveness of sins.

This is an altar call where nothing is asked of us but where as children we are fed. We come and kneel, acknowledging our humility and oneness with the earth (humus). Our hands open to receive remind us of our poverty and need. Our eyes closed in prayer signal our blindness which needs to be healed. Or we may do none of these things—our actions are not the important point here.

The important thing is that we are nourished by communing with the one to whom we are bound in baptism. Here again our old self is pushed down toward death and a new self is nourished. The benefits are the same as in baptism—forgiveness of sins, life, and salvation—and the means are similar: words of promise accompanying earthly elements—then water, now bread and wine. God himself breaks through to us in a saving way in, with, and under earthly signs.

At God's altar call the word of promise is particularized and focused in eating and drinking, that is, in tangible, physical materials external to us so that there can be no doubt that it is meant for us, for you and for me. I may doubt that the spoken announcement of the gospel of forgiveness is really meant for me, but it is not doubtful when the bread and wine go down my throat, just as it was not doubtful when I was washed with the waters of baptism. At this meal we receive the visible, touchable, edible Word of God's love for us. It is not a different word from God's other words, but it is one personalized for each one of us—so that we may believe it and trust it with our whole heart.

It is important to stress the faith-creating and faith-sustaining character of this meal, for that is what makes it a redemptive meal. Trusting the promises of God makes us truly human, truly the creatures we were meant to be, truly in the image of God as revealed by Jesus Christ himself. This sacrament does not exalt us to heaven but anchors us to earth—where we are meant to be. It does this by creating in us the same things that happened to Jesus Christ—by enabling us to lose our lives for his sake, by having his death take place in us so that his resurrection might give us hope and newness of life now. We remember the events of his life and take them inside of ourselves by eating and drinking and hearing so that his history might be ours as well, for his way is the only way to true life.

But questions arise. How is Jesus present in this sacrament? Is he not in heaven at God's right hand? God's right hand is not a place, for God is not bound to our limitations of time and space. His "right hand" is simply a symbol of his power —Jesus is united with God's creating and redeeming power.

Well, then, does something happen to the bread and wine to turn them into Christ's body and blood? Sometimes Christians have spoken as if that were so, but there is nothing in the Bible to support the idea of a change. Rather, in Matthew, Mark, Luke, and 1 Corinthians it says that Jesus took *bread* and gave thanks and gave *it* to them and said, "This is my body." It is similar for the wine. Martin Luther reminded the church to focus not on *how* this could be the case but to concentrate on Jesus' words which promise that this bread is his body and this wine is his blood. If Jesus is one with God the Father, who creates and is part of everything and who is everywhere present, then Jesus shares in these traits of God. So the difficulty is not with how Christ can be in the bread and wine. The difficulty is in our trusting that he is there for us and for our salvation—as the words promise. The main point is not his presence but his mercy—that is, his presence *for us*. It is in his *saving* presence in this sacrament that we believe on the basis of Christ's promise. That is why the pastor always repeats Christ's words which began this supper—so that we may hear them as Christ's promise and believe as we eat and drink.

Does it all depend on my faith then? By no means! It depends on Christ's promise. My faith will never be pure or wholly sincere. If it depended on my faith, then this would not be a meal of assurance and joy but of anxiety and fear. The validity of the Lord's Supper does not depend on the faith of the recipient. Rather, the recipient's faith is the goal of this sacrament. Faith is something God's Spirit creates in us (indeed, no one can even say "Jesus is Lord" except by the Holy Spirit—1 Cor. 12:3). Christ is present in the bread and wine and he is present there for us and for our salvation because he promises to be there—whether or not we believe it. Our faith is to be aroused and nourished precisely by hearing Christ's promise to be there for us. Thus everyone who eats and drinks the bread and wine receives Christ—though if we do so not believing his promises it is certainly not to our benefit.

Well, if everything depends on the words of promise from the Bible, could I simply read my Bible at home and eat bread and drink wine and have the sacrament without going to church? Conceivably there have been and will be extreme circumstances where such a thing might happen, but it risks having us forget the communal nature of Christian faith as well

as the idea that this is a family meal. This is why we try to
link Communion services for shut-in people or those in the
hospital to the Sunday worship of the whole congregation by
having other members of the family or the congregation present or by bringing a recording of the worship service. The
most important Bible passage here is 1 Corinthians 11:17-34,
where the point is made that not only do we receive Christ's
body and blood but at the same time we *are* his body now on
earth (see also 1 Cor. 10:16-17; 12:12-13). The purpose of
God's feeding us and giving us faith is to build his scattered
and warring people back together again. Thus, ordinarily, the
Lord's Supper is a service for the whole congregation—it is a
Holy *Communion*, with God and with all others who are part
of Christ's body. Here, too, we cannot be Christians alone.

Free Lunch

The familiar saying puts it: "There is no such thing as a
free lunch." It refers to the fact that in everyday life few
things are done without regard to self-interest. When someone offers to give us something for nothing we get suspicious
because we know that people just don't do that. There is no
such thing as a free lunch without strings attached. Accept a
"free" lunch and you will be expected to sign a contract, or
to buy insurance, or to go to bed, or to do a favor, or to do
something else you had not wanted to do.

Thus it is hard to believe it when we hear that while we
were still weak, Christ died for us (Rom. 5:6-11). Why, one
will hardly die for a righteous person, though perhaps, in
certain circumstances, one would do that. But God shows his
love for us in that while we were yet sinners, Christ died for
us. That's hard to believe. What's the catch? What does God

want from me? Aha! Here it comes: *Since,* therefore, we are
now justified by his blood . . . . You just know God expects
something in return.

But God crosses us up again. All it says (still in Rom. 5)
is that since we are justified, much more shall we be saved
from his wrath. For if when we were enemies we were reconciled to God by the death of his Son, much more, now that
we are reconciled, shall we be saved by his life. Where's the
catch? There has to be a catch. This sounds too good to be
true. We had better check the fine print.

Yet in all the fine print that follows this crucial passage,
the talk continues about this "free gift" which God gives us
—this justification, this eternal life in Christ Jesus our Lord.
Are God's ways different from our ways? You bet. Even as
he was about to die, Christ gave: eternal life to the thief, a
new son for his mother, forgiveness for his executioners.

So too, on the night he was betrayed, he took bread and
gave it; he took wine and *gave* it, for the forgiveness of sins.
You can be sure about this: at least in this one case, there *is*
such a thing as a free lunch. It is the Lord's Supper.

God doesn't want something from us in this meal. He
wants something *for* us—thus he gives. That is why, though
reverence and repentance are of course important, so is joy.
We rightly speak of "celebrating" this sacrament, and we
surround our reception of the bread and wine with hymns and
prayers of praise and thanksgiving, recalling the marvelous
deeds of the God we know in Christ.

"He Who Has Seen Me Has Seen the Father"

Perhaps you noticed that in the above paragraphs Jesus
Christ and God the Father were used almost interchangeably.

Did you wonder about this? It would seem natural to question how one can speak of the eternal creator God as one and the same with Jesus the carpenter from Nazareth. Yet the claim of Christians from the time of Jesus on is that if we know Christ we know God. And you can see how it is essential for Jesus to be one with God if we are to believe that he is present in the bread and wine of the Lord's Supper. None of us could be present in that way.

If we begin with a definition of God such as that he (or she) is all-powerful, all-knowing, all seeing, righteous, holy, invisible, eternal, and unchanging (to list some of the most common ways of defining God in all cultures and at all times), then it will be difficult or even impossible to see how the man Jesus is all or any of those things. What the Bible does, however, is to suggest that we not start with a prior definition of God but that we start with Jesus. We must learn to think of God only in Jesus Christ. Then we will not stress the abstract characteristics listed previously. Instead, we will talk about God as the one who is loving and forgiving, as Jesus was, and who is faithful and unwavering in his purpose to save his people. When we confess that Jesus is truly divine we aren't saying that Jesus fits some definition of what it is to be divine but that what it is to be divine is to be what Jesus is. Compare this to what was said earlier in this book: that to say that Jesus is truly human is not to say he is just like us but to admit that in our sin we are subhuman and Jesus is what we are meant to be.

We are to start thinking about our faith from the point of the one who saved us by grace through faith, for he is the truth about God and about everything else. We know everything there is to know about God when we know Jesus Christ.

When we think about Jesus specifically in the Lord's Supper we know that God is a God who loves us and wills to be part of us and make us part of himself and his body. He is a God who comes to us in concrete ways—preeminently in the man Jesus crucified and risen, and still in bread and wine, water and word, and in those who are in need. He is a God who comes to us from outside us, as Jesus did. He is external to us and uses external means to reach us so that we may be freed from our own internal self-centeredness and may be justified by a word from outside us—for by our own words and works none of us will be saved. He is a God who has made this world and all of us and who loves everything that he has made, so that he gives his life for us. He is a God who even on the day of judgment will be one with Jesus Christ, so that we may not fear but have hope.

It is this God to whom we bear witness, even as we eat the bread and drink the wine, for when we do this we proclaim the *death* of Christ until he comes again (1 Cor. 11:26). In the death of Christ we see supremely into the loving heart of God, who did not spare his own Son, but gave him up for us all (Rom. 8:32).

In the Lord's Supper, by giving us faith, God anchors us firmly in the created order by our receiving and by our community so that we will serve him there by serving our fellow creatures. Precisely by being so anchored and grounded we proclaim the saving death of Christ until he comes again. We will think about the end-time in our final chapter.

For further reading:

Forde, Gerhard—*Where God Meets Man,* Chapter 5
Gritsch, Eric & Jenson, Robert—*Lutheranism,* Chapters 6 and 7
Jenson, Robert—*Visible Words*

Knutson, Kent—*His Only Son Our Lord*
Vajta, Vilmos—*Luther on Worship*

QUESTIONS FOR DISCUSSION

1. What standards do you think should be used to decide who should receive the Lord's Supper? Why?
2. Should you receive Communion even if you are mixed up or uncertain about your own faith?
3. On what basis do you think the frequency of the celebration and reception of this sacrament should be decided?
4. If it is the *Lord's* Supper, what might that suggest about denominational differences in explaining and limiting participation in this sacrament?
5. What are the most important things that we need to remember about the Lord's Supper? What are some things related to the Supper that really are secondary?

13 · Standing on the Promises

Blessed be the God and Father of our Lord Jesus Christ! By his great mercy we have been born anew to a living hope through the resurrection of Jesus Christ from the dead, and to an inheritance which is imperishable, undefiled, and unfading, kept in heaven for you, who by God's power are guarded through faith for a salvation ready to be revealed in the last time.

1 PETER 1:3-5

The Bible's language about the future and heaven and eternal salvation is hard for us to understand today. It has been the subject of scathing criticism and ridicule, and it has been more subtly undermined by our modern assumptions about the world. Yet modern biblical scholarship has discovered that this "eschatological" (from *eschaton*, the Greek word for the end of time) or futuristic material in the Bible is absolutely essential for understanding the Christian message. Therefore we dare not let it drop out of our consciousness or we will have only part of the story on which our faith is based.

Here we need to make a distinction between our knowledge of the past and present, on the one hand, and our knowledge of the future, on the other. The present and at least the recent past are measurable and touchable and can be or have been experienced. But the future cannot be known in these same ways. When it comes to the future we can dream and hope, or plan and design, or write fiction about it—but we cannot *know* it in the same sense that we can know the past or present.

We need to remember this when we consider the eschatological portions of the Bible. They speak in a different way from most of the other parts of Scripture. If we take them as *explanations* of the future, they may seem absurd or meaningless. But if we see them instead as stories embodying hopes and dreams or as parables attempting to speak of the wonders of heavenly fulfillment while being limited to the language of earthly fulfillments, then we may be able to see that these stories are helpful to us as *explorations* of the future. They probe the ultimate meaning of having our destiny in the God who is the Father of Jesus Christ. They are not predictions but promises. We also need to take them "seriously but not literally."

There are many stories of the future in the literature of the world's religions, but they are not all the same. Thus it is wise for us to look at the specifically Christian stories, not least because we know that the images we have of the future have a decisive effect on our lives in the present. Human beings seek to bring about what they hope for. The hoped-for future shapes our actions and attitudes. The images of the future which our faith gives us are projected onto the future only to ricochet back on us to influence us to bring it about.

Of course, it is not that we alone bring about the eschatological future, nor even that God does it primarily by working through us, though our actions should not be discounted. For the Christian notion of the end portrays it as something new and beyond history, while at the same time being the fulfillment of history. But let us look at the three main images of the future found in the New Testament before drawing any more conclusions.

The Return of Christ

The stories of the return of Christ or the "second coming" are among the most vivid in Scripture. In Acts 1:10-11, two men in white robes tell the disciples: "Men of Galilee, why do you stand looking into heaven? This Jesus . . . will come in the same way as you saw him go into heaven." This image appears in a variety of ways in other places (compare Matt. 25 and 26, John 14, 1 Cor. 15, 2 Thess. 2, and Rev. 20 and 21). While the stories themselves are highly symbolic and puzzling in many ways, their main point is quite straightforward: because of the promised return of Christ we are to live with hope in the present time. This is put most clearly in 1 Corinthians 15:58: "Be steadfast, immovable, always abounding in the work of the Lord, knowing that in the Lord your labor is not in vain." If that were not clear enough, the sentence is preceded by "Therefore," hearkening back to the whole chapter concerning the resurrection of Christ, which is called the "first fruits" of the general resurrection of all people and the return of Christ.

If we study the theme of the return of Christ, we see that it testifies to the cosmic scope of God's judgment and grace—

against any individualism. It also calls into question any belief in progress in our world by its claim that the fulfillment of history lies beyond history. Yet at the same time, against any other wordliness, it says that the consummation fulfills rather than negates the historical process. Jesus returns to this world, after all; he does not meet those who will be saved somewhere else.

The Last Judgment

Closely related to the return of Christ is the idea of the last judgment. It is also portrayed in several places (Matt. 25, 2 Cor. 5, Acts 10, and Rom. 2). Again, if we take this theme or story seriously without taking it literally, many rich meanings come out. The most important is that it is *Christ* who will be the judge. Here *all* the New Testament's testimony to Christ is important. The one who is truly human will judge; and this is the same one who is truly divine. This means that the judgment is on sin and not on our humanness, since it is the one who has taken on our flesh forever who will judge us. God's last judgment will reflect his first judgment on our creatureliness—it is good. It is sin that is the problem.

Note also that in these stories good and evil do not vanish. Apparently being saved by grace alone does not mean that what we do does not matter, as some have thought. Good and evil are part of the final judgment, and even the righteous (the sheep in Matt. 25) are uneasy about their righteousness. This ought not to be surprising, since all have sinned. But it reminds us of the importance of Christ's atoning work. In the Bible evil is not simply erased or ignored, but God reconciles the world to himself by bearing the cost of the world's rebellion himself. Atonement for God is neither easy nor automatic, just as in human relationships forgiving and reconciling are costly and often painful events. The story of the last judgment holds before us the message that what we do now matters, whether good or evil; these things will remain and they will come under judgment.

Finally, the judgment by Jesus is said to come at the end of history, not within it. That is, nothing we achieve or fail to achieve here will have the *last* word. God has the last word. And in the final judgment of our own death, our sin of centering our lives on ourselves will be shown to be an idol. As we see this idol collapse, we will finally be opened to dependence only on God's mercy.

The Resurrection of the Dead

The New Testament speaks throughout of the general resurrection of all who have died when the end comes (see Matt. 22, Luke 14, Rom. 6, 1 Thess. 4, and especially 1 Cor. 15). The first point to be made from these materials is that resurrection is not identical with immortality, because immortality implies that there is something innately eternal about us to which we can hold in death. Against this, resurrection speaks about *new* bodies. This suggests at least two things: eternity will fulfill and not annul human life in the world, since bodies are still spoken of; but also, there is nothing within the human condition itself that can accomplish this fulfillment. Death is real. Only God can perform a resurrection (even Jesus "was raised"), and while we cannot know about this future act of our resurrection in the way we know things in the present, we can trust it because it accords with all that we believe about God who perpetually creates anew. One could say that the resurrection affirms meaning to history in a way similar to creation in the beginning, but now from the other "end."

It is also important to note that both the New Testament and the Apostles' Creed affirm the resurrection of the *body*. Since "body" is the biblical word for the whole person, referring to one's historical identity, we believe that God will value all aspects of our experience. Heaven will not be absorption into God but fellowship with him. If it is taken literally, this idea too may seem absurd. But if it is seen as an exploration into the future of God and his people, it is helpful. It makes more sense of our experience than the view which has the future all spelled out and thus has no way of taking seriously the conditions of present existence or the view that has no future at all beyond death and thus must worship present existence.

The images of the resurrection, the return of Christ, and of the last judgment all function to keep hope alive (this life is not all there is or will be). They also serve to keep the future open (our actions will contribute to it but they alone do not determine it) and preserve the appropriateness of living by faith.

Those who believe that this life is all there is will be tempted to despair when their lives or work turn out to seem meaningless or tragic. Or, if there is no future beyond death, our achievements will seem unimportant and we will be tempted to cynicism. In the face of such alternatives, the eschatological message of Christianity that God will value good and condemn evil encourages our creativity, responsibility, and self-sacrifice. There should be no substance in the charge often made that Christianity's hope for the future devalues present existence; this is true only when the hope is misconstrued as some sort of ironclad prediction which does not take our humanity seriously. It would be better to argue the other way: that a certain hope leads to a dynamic involvement in the present. An example of this is seen in the Puritans, who believed in predestination and who worked hard precisely because of their certainty of salvation. As has been said, "he fights hardest who fights for a predestined victory." Or, as in an athletic contest which has turned into a rout: the team which knows it is going to win suddenly can do nothing wrong.

If we don't take the long run into account, we will misunderstand the short run and burn ourselves out or go in wrong directions. As someone has said, "If you don't know where you're going, any road will get you there." Christian faith looks at the future not with the certainty of a map but with the reliability of a compass, with urgency and yet without panic, and with a hope that sustains us as creatures and children of God our Maker and Redeemer.

In baptism we are born anew to a *living hope*. Objectively, that living hope is the risen Lord Jesus Christ. Subjectively, it is the hopefulness aroused in us by the Holy Spirit. We are *called* to hope (Eph. 4:4); in fact, faith is our assurance of those things for which we *hope* (Heb. 11:1).

This hope we have in Christ is God's power which is at work in us causing us to live now in accordance with the promised future—even when that involves suffering or conflict with the present. We have a new itinerary in which true life follows death. God calls all people to this journey. Precisely when things are not going well, our hope may be contagious. Other people may be infected by our hope and come with us to meet the crucified and risen Lord who calls us all into his future. Amen. Come, Lord Jesus!

Nothing that is worth doing can be achieved in our lifetime; therefore we must be saved by hope. Nothing which is true or beautiful or good makes complete sense in any immediate context of history; therefore we must be saved by faith. Nothing we do, however virtuous, can be accomplished alone; therefore we must be saved by love. No virtuous act is quite as virtuous from the standpoint of our friend or foe as it is from our standpoint; therefore we must be saved by the final form of love which is forgiveness.

—REINHOLD NIEBUHR

For further reading:

Capps, Walter H.—*Time Invades the Cathedral*
Niebuhr, Reinhold—*The Nature and Destiny of Man*, Vol. II, Chapter 10
Peters, Ted—*Fear, Faith, and the Future*
Robinson, John A. T.—*In the End, God*
Stendahl, Krister, ed.,—*Resurrection and Immortality*

QUESTIONS FOR DISCUSSION

1. Do you find it helpful to think of the Bible's language about the future as exploratory rather than explanatory? As promises rather than predictions? Why or why not?

2. The Bible's words about judgment are interpreted above as threats to make us realize our guilt and open us to God's mercy now—before the end. What do you think about this?

3. The Christian faith does not give us a map of all the details about the future but it gives us a compass—pointing toward the God who is also Lord of the future. Do you find that this encourages you to live responsibly more than the views of some Christians who think each detail of the future can be found in the Bible? Discuss.